Evenin

Evening Prayers

For Every Day of the Year

Christoph Friedrich Blumhardt

PLOUGH PUBLISHING HOUSE

Published by Plough Publishing House
Walden, New York
Robertsbridge, East Sussex
Elsmore, Australia
www.plough.com

Original Title: *Abendgebete für alle Tage des Jahres*, Furche Verlag, Berlin, 1926;
second edition: Gotthelf Verlag, Zurich, n.d. Used with permission.
Translated and edited from the German by Plough Publishing House.

Illustrations by Marcus and Rita Wegner

1st edition 1971
2nd edition 1972
3rd edition 1988 entitled *Lift Thine Eyes*
4th edition 1998 entitled *Lift Thine Eyes*
5th edition 2014
Softcover edition 2016

SOFTCOVER ISBN: 978-0-87486-097-9

A catalog record for this book is available from the British Library.
Library of Congress Cataloging-in-Publication Data for hardcover edition

Blumhardt, Christoph, 1842-1919.
[Abendgebete für alle Tage des Jahres. English]
Evening prayers : for every day of the year / Christoph Friedrich Blumhardt. -- 5th edition.
pages cm
ISBN 978-0-87486-811-1 (hardcover)
1. Prayers. 2. Devotional calendars. I. Title.
BV247.B5813 2014
242'.2--dc23

2013049774

You who answer prayer, to you all people will come.

PSALM 65:2

To the Reader

What is it about these evening prayers that still draws thousands of people around the world to turn to them daily, a century after they were spoken? Their rare simplicity and authority spring from the remarkable life of their author, Christoph Friedrich Blumhardt, a pastor and theologian who influenced Dietrich Bonhoeffer, Paul Tillich, and Karl Barth. As Barth writes of Blumhardt's approach to prayer: "Our cause, our hope, is served better with prayers than with treatises...If we want to become healthy and strong, we have to start from the beginning and become like children. That is where Blumhardt can be of great service to people everywhere."

This modern spiritual classic, now in a newly revised edition, is introduced below by Eugen Jäckh, a friend of Blumhardt's and the editor of his complete works.

Originally intended only for some of Blumhardt's close friends, this book of prayers was collected after his death in 1919. Taken from evening devotions that Blumhardt held at Bad Boll, in Germany, these prayers were said without any thought of publication. The fact that they came into being out of real life in this way has endeared them to many who have since used them. The style of the prayers has been changed as little as possible in order to maintain the quality of the spoken word and their essential simplicity.

Those who knew Blumhardt were deeply impressed by the pastoral, even priestly, quality of his personality. His concern went out not only to those whom he knew or who sought his help, but to the whole world. He prayed "without ceasing," but not with many words. He stood before God, mindful of people and their needs and answerable for them.

People's concerns were important to him because, for him, they were God's concerns. It is characteristic of him that when he prayed, the first three requests of the Lord's Prayer always rose involuntarily to his lips. He lived in them and subordinated everything else to them. "All we ask and long for, all our concerns down to the very smallest, we lay in your hands in the one great request that your name be glorified on earth as it is in heaven." Blumhardt's short, concentrated prayers contain everything that we want to bring before God, though he never gets lost in details and trivialities. His whole being, and therefore his praying as well, is ruled completely by the saying: "Seek first the kingdom of God and his righteousness, and all these things will be given to you as well" (Matt. 6:33). Because of this, we seldom hear him ask for these other things.

Blumhardt's prayers breathe forth peace in a remarkable way; they have no overwrought emotionalism about them. This peace comes from Blumhardt's unshakable conviction that God's kingdom is on the way in spite of stormy and changing times. And so he gives thanks "for giving our hearts hope for your kingdom, the kingdom of God. We thank you that again and again we may draw strength from this hope, find new youthfulness and courage, and discover how powerfully, though hidden, your kingdom is already approaching." But because his heart trembles within him, like the hearts of all those who are waiting for this coming of God's kingdom, he asks, "in order that God can speak to us," for the "quietness we need in order to stand before God and forget all the things that can assail us."

Just as nearly every letter of Paul begins with thanks, so Blumhardt too in his prayers is always full of praise and thanks. For there is nothing that can lighten our hearts like giving thanks. In giving thanks we are positive; in the face of thanks everything negative and contrary disappears. Blumhardt's thanksgiving does not lose itself in details and superficialities, but is completely directed towards the most inward and central thing that is given to us by God – that we are his children. Therefore Blumhardt never tires of giving his simple, childlike thanks that God is our Father and that we may be his children.

But "if children, then heirs, heirs of God and fellow heirs with Christ, provided we suffer with him in order that we may also be glorified with him" (Rom. 8:17). Blumhardt's prayers flow out of this feeling for the suffering of the whole world. But there is no sighing about them – they are strong and glad and confident of victory in the knowledge of God's promise, which has been given us. Basically they all point in the same direction – to the prayer that God's kingdom shall come, that the Savior shall come. If we pray, all sin and need can only strengthen our faith in the certainty of God's promise that he will complete his work and bring an end to all affliction.

Eugen Jäckh

January

1

January

This, then, is how you should pray: "Our Father in heaven, hallowed be your name, your kingdom come, your will be done, on earth as it is in heaven."

MATTHEW 6:9–10

Our Father in heaven, may your name be honored. May your kingdom come and your will be done on earth as in heaven. May this continue to be our prayer in the new year, and may we find fellowship with one another in what is eternal and holy. Bless us on our way. Bless us on our earthly pilgrimage so that we may remain free from all bondage, able to thank you day and night for all the good you do, even when things look very dark. We praise your name and we pray as the Savior has taught us. Amen.

2

January

For this reason I bow my knees before the Father, from whom every family in heaven and on earth takes its name. I pray that, according to the riches of his glory, he may grant that you may be strengthened in your inner being with power through his Spirit, and that Christ may dwell in your hearts through faith, as you are being rooted and grounded in love. EPHESIANS 3:14–17, NRSV

Lord our God, we have gathered in your sight. We thank you that through your words you have given something of your very self to help us be your disciples, your children, who stand firm in faith and trust throughout our lives, whatever our lot may be. Help us in these times, and when days grow difficult and full of grief, hold your people securely in your hand. Help us to be firmly rooted in faith, however dark it is on earth. You can give us strength and courage; we can do nothing in our human strength. But the power of your Spirit can renew us, make us alert, and fill us with lasting joy. For we are your people, your children, and when held in your hand, we can rejoice in spite of all grief. Amen.

3

January

The Lord has made proclamation to the ends of the earth: "Say to Daughter Zion, 'See, your Savior comes! See, his reward is with him, and his recompense accompanies him.'" ISAIAH 62:11

Lord our God, we thank you that we may go to meet you with open hearts, with jubilant faith, and with this joyful shout, "God's salvation is coming! Through Jesus Christ day is dawning on earth for all nations." Stay with us and help us. Send us your Spirit to strengthen us, especially in times of trouble. Let all nations come before you. Let us tell all peoples, "Be comforted. The salvation of our God, who is also your God, is coming. In this salvation we will rejoice together forevermore to the glory of our God." Amen.

4

January

He said to me, "You are my servant, Israel, in whom I will display my splendor." But I said, "I have labored in vain; I have spent my strength for nothing at all. Yet what is due me is in the Lord's hand, and my reward is with my God." ISAIAH 49:3–4

Lord our God, we thank you for the help you have given us over and over again so that we can stand before you, rejoicing in the certainty of faith. We thank you for guiding and leading our lives and for letting us see a goal ahead, a goal to be revealed to all people. Be with us in times of silence when we seem to be alone. Keep us strong and steadfast through temptation and through all the turmoil of life. Help us to remain unshaken, for you walk with us holding us by the hand, and you can lift us above all that does not endure. Amen.

5
January

The people living in darkness have seen a great light; on those living in the land of the shadow of death a light has dawned. MATTHEW 4:16

Dear Father in heaven, be close to us as we seek you in the quiet of our hearts. Grant us the strength of your Spirit, the strength to wait patiently for your help in our lives. Help us to hold to all that is good. Help us to feel, each one of us, that we are your children and that we may rejoice in your fatherly care. May your will be done more and more fully in us and around us. May your will be done so that we may be given ever greater freeing and your light can dawn where there is still darkness. Amen.

6

January

After Jesus was born in Bethlehem in Judea, during the time of King Herod, Magi from the east came to Jerusalem and asked, "Where is the one who has been born king of the Jews? We saw his star when it rose and have come to worship him." MATTHEW 2:1–2

Lord our God, we thank you that you have come to this earth. Let a light shine out again and again among those who hear your gospel, also among those with sincere hearts, whether or not they are Christians. May they come to know your light and receive salvation in Jesus Christ. May your light shine for us and may you appear to us ever more clearly. Remember all who call to you. Remember your people. May your people gather and become a light in your name, serving you wherever they go. Amen.

7

January

Arise, shine, for your light has come, and the glory of the Lord rises upon you. See, darkness covers the earth and thick darkness is over the peoples, but the Lord rises upon you and his glory appears over you. Nations will come to your light, and kings to the brightness of your dawn. ISAIAH 60:1–3

Dear Father in heaven, accept us as your children, whose lives are under your protection and who turn to you for strength. In the midst of all the struggles and temptations in this world keep us certain of your love and goodness. Grant that we may help your name to be honored on earth and your salvation to spread over all the world. May we help that the hope you have given us brings light and strength for our own lives and for all whom you love in Jesus Christ. Amen.

8

January

The apostles said to the Lord, "Increase our faith!" He replied, "If you have faith as small as a mustard seed, you can say to this mulberry tree, 'Be uprooted and planted in the sea,' and it will obey you." LUKE 17:5–6

Father in heaven, we thank you for the many ways you strengthen us and reveal your life to us. We thank you for all your protection, also for your protection of our faith and hope. Grant that your Spirit may penetrate us more and more, enabling us to be your witnesses in this evil and unhappy world. May your Spirit give us hope for this life and for the life to come. Amen.

9
January

But thanks be to God! He gives us the victory through our Lord Jesus Christ. Therefore, my dear brothers and sisters, stand firm. Let nothing move you. Always give yourselves fully to the work of the Lord, because you know that your labor in the Lord is not in vain.

1 CORINTHIANS 15:57–58

Lord our God, we thank you that we are allowed to live in your love. We thank you for your promise that all the suffering on earth shall come to an end. Hear us when we turn to you with all we have on our hearts. We are weak, but you are strong. May we hope and trust in your strength. May our life, with all its practical concerns, remain in your hands until the day when you will act in might and the whole world will know the forgiveness of sins and will praise and thank you evermore. Amen.

10

January

Comfort, comfort my people, says your God. Speak tenderly to Jerusalem, and proclaim to her that her hard service has been completed, that her sin has been paid for, that she has received from the Lord's hand double for all her sins. ISAIAH 40:1–2

Lord our God, how great is your love, and how great is your help! May each one of us feel sheltered in your hand, knowing that our faults and shortcomings no longer matter. We can go straight toward the goal you have set, for you will help us through the forgiveness of sins and through all the good you can put into our hearts. And so we ask you to be with us. May we be faithful, believing firmly in your great mercy, so that your name may be glorified among us. May each heart be given the comfort of knowing that everything will yet turn to the good, to the glory of your name. Amen.

11

January

The Lord is my light and my salvation – whom shall I fear? The Lord is the stronghold of my life – of whom shall I be afraid? PSALM 27:1

Our dear Father, we ask you to come to us from heaven and surround us with your goodness and mercy, with your light and life. We are weak, poor, and lost just when we need to stand firm and hold on. But you are faithful. You stay by us and help us. Continue to help and sustain us, we pray. Do not let our lives be lived in vain. May something of eternity be with us in all we have to face in life, so that over and over again we may find courage to start anew. Amen.

12

January

Cast your cares on the Lord and he will sustain you; he will never let the righteous be shaken. PSALM 55:22

Dear Father in heaven, you let us see and feel your great goodness toward us. Grant us the inner help to be victorious in the Savior, rejoicing to be by his side with faith and loyalty, and with the strength of soul that frees us from all burdens by laying them in your hands. Hear us as together we pray to you. All we ask and long for, all our concerns down to the very smallest, we lay in your hands in the one great request that your name be glorified on earth as it is in heaven. Amen.

13

January

Be on your guard; stand firm in the faith; be courageous; be strong. Do everything in love.

I CORINTHIANS 16:13–14

Dear Father in heaven, give us childlike hearts so that we may understand everything in the right way. Grant us work that bears fruit in spite of our faults and weaknesses, because we want to work with the understanding given by love. Father in heaven, you know that we are faced day and night with many difficulties and setbacks. But you see us, and you will help us so that your name may be honored, your kingdom may come, and your will may be done on earth as in heaven. Amen.

14

January

For to be sure, he was crucified in weakness, yet he lives by God's power. Likewise, we are weak in him, yet by God's power we will live with him to serve you.

2 CORINTHIANS 13:4

Lord our God, we come into your presence and kneel before your throne, asking you with all our hearts for your Spirit, so that our lives may be guided and ruled by you, the one God and Creator of all life. Let your Word come into our hearts. Give your blessing on all we experience in life and on all we ask of you as we stand before you. We are weak and poor. We can achieve nothing, and our hearts are weary. But you can strengthen us. You can make everything come right to reveal your kingdom throughout the world. Then all the people of our time may come to know that your will for the earth is not distress and suffering, but your goodness, your life, and your eternity. Amen.

15

January

Likewise the Spirit helps us in our weakness; for we do not know how to pray as we ought, but that very Spirit intercedes with sighs too deep for words.

ROMANS 8:26, NRSV

Lord God, send your Spirit, we pray, over us and over the whole world. Let your light dawn on earth among humankind. Reveal your power and let your reign begin. May your will be done, O Lord. We kneel before your throne and plead to you. We are weak. Lord, help us. Bless us. Establish your kingdom in the hearts of those who are willing to follow you, who are willing to accept your grace in Jesus Christ. Help us through your strength. Reign over us. Be with us with your Holy Spirit, O Lord God, our Father. Amen.

16

January

I will exalt you, my God the King; I will praise your name for ever and ever. Every day I will praise you and extol your name for ever and ever. PSALM 145:1–2

Dear Father in heaven, we come before you and thank you with all our hearts. You know all that we are thankful for. Continue to sustain us, we pray, and give us strength for the paths on which you lead us. Even when we must suffer and fight long, hard battles, we know that everything has its right purpose and will still lead us to your goal. For all this we praise and thank you. Protect us in mind, heart, and spirit. Keep us courageous, and lift us above all discouragement through your Spirit, who will renew our lives forevermore. Amen.

17

January

The Lord is my shepherd, I lack nothing. He makes me lie down in green pastures, he leads me beside quiet waters, he refreshes my soul. He guides me along the right paths for his name's sake. PSALM 23:1–3

Dear Father in heaven, we thank you that we need never feel forsaken. We thank you that we are led and guided by your hand. We thank you for all we have received from you, your care for our bodies, for our material needs, and for our inner life. We praise you, O God! Continue to lead us, we pray. Continue to work among us so that we can all see and come to know that the Good Shepherd is leading us. Amen.

18

January

Consider it pure joy, my brothers and sisters, whenever you face trials of many kinds...Blessed is the one who perseveres under trial because, having stood the test, that person will receive the crown of life that the Lord has promised to those who love him. JAMES 1:2,12

Lord our God, be with us. Touch us with your Spirit so that our hearts may receive something from you. Let us find joy even in a life of struggle and temptation. Let us find joy in every need we face, even in the agony of death. Protect us through your Word, and let it always be a light to us so that we can follow you and do your will. Be with us on all our ways. Guide everything with your hand until the goal for all humankind is reached and we may rejoice over all the trials and testing because in the end the glorious prize can be won. Amen.

19

January

But you are our Father, though Abraham does not know us or Israel acknowledge us; you, Lord, are our Father, our Redeemer from of old is your name. ISAIAH 63:16

Lord God, we thank you as we look back to the times throughout the ages when your servants lifted a voice to witness that you are our Father, that you lead the peoples to their true goal. However long it may take, we thank you for allowing us to be part of this witness. We thank you that so much love and goodness still shine into our time as a light to the nations. Watch over us. May your Spirit grow stronger and stronger within us. Bring the redemption proclaimed by your servants, and let your light dawn over all lands to the honor of your name. Amen.

20
January

So do not fear, for I am with you; do not be dismayed, for I am your God. I will strengthen you and help you; I will uphold you with my righteous right hand. ISAIAH 41:10

Dear Father in heaven, we thank you that you are our Father and that we may have you with us. We thank you that we can know you are leading us by your hand. Give us your Spirit of understanding so that we may always see your mighty and powerful hand guiding us on all our ways. Help us where we fall short. Help us, for we are weak and are often in situations where we cannot help ourselves. But you are strong. You give light to our hearts. Through the Savior, Jesus Christ, we can direct our lives cheerfully, joyfully, and patiently toward the great goal set before us your children, and before the whole world. Amen.

21
January

In my distress I called to the Lord; I cried to my God for help. From his temple he heard my voice; my cry came before him, into his ears. PSALM 18:6

Dear Father in heaven, we rejoice that you are our Father. We rejoice that you rule and guide each of us so that our path in life leads to what is good and genuine and we do not get stuck in this or that concern. Lead us, renew us, and again and again free us to go forward, finding new courage and joy for ourselves and for our fellowmen. Then we can praise you, your strength and power can be revealed to us, your heaven come down to earth, and your will be done on earth. Here on earth your help shall come to the poor, the weak, the lowly, the sick, and the suffering. May your name be praised! We rejoice in your name. Amen.

22
January

Come to me, all you who are weary and burdened, and I will give you rest. MATTHEW 11:28

Dear Father in heaven, grant us the inner quiet we need so that we may come into your presence and hear you speak, forgetting all the things that try to force themselves upon us. May we experience your true and living support. Keep our hearts glad and thankful for everything, even in grief, anxiety, and suffering. In this thankfulness we can remain with you, and Jesus Christ can help us, Jesus, whom you have given as our support and helper in all that most deeply concerns us. We entrust ourselves to you. Keep us in your Spirit. Amen.

23
January

The Lord has established his throne in heaven, and his kingdom rules over all...Praise the Lord, all his works everywhere in his dominion. Praise the Lord, my soul.

PSALM 103:19, 22

Dear Father in heaven, we thank you for giving our hearts hope for your kingdom, the kingdom of God. We thank you that again and again we may draw strength from this hope, find new youthfulness and courage, and discover how powerfully, though hidden, your kingdom is already approaching. Protect this vision and help us when we fail. All will come right. Whatever happens, we are in your hands, and no one shall snatch this joy from our hearts. Amen.

24

January

I have not spoken in secret, from somewhere in a land of darkness; I have not said to Jacob's descendants, "Seek me in vain." I, the Lord, speak the truth; I declare what is right. ISAIAH 45:19

Lord our God, we thank you for giving us your love, for letting us draw nearer to what is right and good. May your Spirit penetrate everywhere, overcoming what is false and helping people everywhere to understand the true nature of your justice. Guard us on all our ways. Protect us when our bodies and our lives are worn down by sickness and distress of every kind. Grant us your help according to your truth and righteousness. Amen.

25

January

You are the light of the world. A town built on a hill cannot be hidden. Neither do people light a lamp and put it under a bowl. Instead they put it on its stand, and it gives light to everyone in the house. In the same way, let your light shine before others, that they may see your good deeds and glorify your Father in heaven.

MATTHEW 5:14–16

Lord our God, O God of righteousness, let your light shine out. Go with us on our way. May we have clear eyes and hearts through your Word and your Spirit. Through temptations and struggles be always with us, lighting our way to what is right and good. Protect and bless us. Move our hearts from their very depths to thank you for all you have done for us, to praise you, and to glorify you. Amen.

26

January

The Lord is near to all who call on him, to all who call on him in truth. He fulfills the desires of those who fear him; he hears their cry and saves them. PSALM 145:18–19

Dear Father in heaven, Almighty God, your children look to you in prayer. Hold us always by the hand. Reveal to us that you hear us, that you are among us providing what is best for us, to the glory of your name. In this hour let us experience something from you, the good and merciful One. May we always be glad and thankful for all we have already received from you and for all we are still to receive in our lives. Amen.

27
January

And this is my prayer: that your love may abound more and more in knowledge and depth of insight, so that you may be able to discern what is best and may be pure and blameless for the day of Christ, filled with the fruit of righteousness that comes through Jesus Christ – to the glory and praise of God. PHILIPPIANS 1:9–11

Lord our God, we thank you for filling our hearts with such great trust. We thank you for all we are given in our lives, above all that we can come to know Jesus Christ. We thank you that over and over we can draw strength and life from his life. Praise to your name, for our life has a goal and we may find strength and certainty during our time on earth. You will reveal what we hope for, and even now you allow us to keep something of this goal before our eyes. We praise you that your name may become great in our midst and that again and again new life can well up from us, who are poor and weak. May your name be praised for setting this goal before us to strengthen us. Amen.

28

January

I will instruct you and teach you in the way you should go; I will counsel you with my loving eye on you.

PSALM 32:8

Lord our God, we come into your presence and ask you to help us. Help us in every part of our lives, even when we do not understand. Be with us with your Spirit. Guide and lead us with your hand. Let your will be done in all things, even if we must bear suffering. Your will is for good alone and you will set everything right. Help us. Bless us through your Word, through everything we are allowed to hear from you, our God and our Father. Amen.

29
January

Hear, O Israel: The Lord our God, the Lord is one. Love the Lord your God with all your heart and with all your soul and with all your strength. These commandments that I give you today are to be on your hearts.

DEUTERONOMY 6:4–6

Lord our God, we thank you that every day – through good days and through days that to us seem bad – we know that our lives are guided by your will, what you do and what you want. For this we thank you. We want to love you above everything in the world. Our hearts long for you, for you are our Father. We want to love and honor you with our whole lives. Lord our God, bring your order into the world. Help us at all times to do your will and to fulfill your commandments. Amen.

30

January

Turn to me and be saved, all you ends of the earth; for I am God, and there is no other. By myself I have sworn, my mouth has uttered in all integrity a word that will not be revoked: Before me every knee will bow; by me every tongue will swear. ISAIAH 45:22–23

Lord God, we kneel before you and worship you, for you do mighty deeds in heaven and on earth and allow us to become your children and your servants. You have done great things for many people, enabling them to serve you, and you will do still more. For you have promised that all our paths will be made straight. You have promised that all we do may be a service to you through Jesus Christ, the Savior of the world, whom we follow. He will be revealed to the whole world, so that the nations will be called to serve you and your will may be done on earth as in heaven. Praised be your name, Lord our God! We open our hearts to you. In death and in life we are yours. Amen.

31
January

For Zion's sake I will not keep silent, for Jerusalem's sake I will not remain quiet, till her vindication shines out like the dawn, her salvation like a blazing torch. ISAIAH 62:1

Lord our God, we worship you, for you come to meet us everywhere and you reveal your glory on our earth. May we become worthy of you, people who can represent you with our whole being. Give us the strength to endure, even through struggles and temptations. Be merciful to us at all times through Jesus Christ our Savior. May we remain body and soul in his hands, that at last we may come to you, our Father in heaven, as your true children, reborn through the Holy Spirit. Amen.

February

1

February

See what great love the Father has lavished on us, that we should be called children of God! And that is what we are! The reason the world does not know us is that it did not know him. 1 JOHN 3:1

Lord our God, we thank you that we may be your children and may be led by your hand. Give us patience and faith, especially when our way on earth seems difficult and life is full of grief and hardship. You are light. You show us the right path. You go before us in the self-denial and patience taught us by your Word. Protect us on all our ways. May your kingdom grow among us until it can be plainly seen that you, O God, are truly with us doing your work and bringing us joy, even though what we do seems fruitless. But your work endures. In your work we rejoice, and we want to give thanks to you every day. Amen.

2

February

And those the Lord has rescued will return. They will enter Zion with singing; everlasting joy will crown their heads. Gladness and joy will overtake them, and sorrow and sighing will flee away. ISAIAH 35:10

Dear Father in heaven, we thank you that you lead us on all our paths. Together we praise your name. We plead with you, stay with us, especially when the world grows darker. Stay with us and send down your power. Send your power in answer to our prayers. For all people we pray, "Father in heaven, these are our brothers and sisters in spite of their failures and sins." Help them, O God. May they soon come to recognize who you are, what you do, and what you will still do, so that the whole world can be joyful and all people on earth may know the blessing of being your children. Amen.

3

February

So in Christ Jesus you are all children of God through faith, for all of you who were baptized into Christ have clothed yourselves with Christ. GALATIANS 3:26–27

Dear Father in heaven, we may come to you, for you have counted us as your children. Our hearts long to come to you, our God and Savior. May your Word bless us and restore us. Give us courageous hearts to bear the distress of our times. Let a light arise in our days so that people care about your will. Then the need on earth shall come to an end, your name shall be honored, and your will be done. Lord God, you alone are our help. Be merciful to us. Stretch out your hand so that all people may turn to you and to your commandments, and your will may be done on earth. Amen.

4
February

Jesus answered, "I am the way and the truth and the life. No one comes to the Father except through me."

JOHN 14:6

Lord our God, help us who have listened in the name of Jesus Christ and heard the good tidings. Help us come with our whole hearts to the Savior, who leads us into your arms. Hear our pleading and let your countenance shine over the world. Let a new age come soon. Send your salvation into the world to the glory of your name, so that the truth we have learned about you becomes a reality in our hearts and our whole life can be genuine, rooted in the truth, leading us into heaven, to the honor of your name. Hear us, O Lord our God. We entrust ourselves and our daily lives to you. We want to be faithful. Help us to be your children, mindful at every step that we belong to you. Amen.

5

February

I will give thanks to you, Lord, with all my heart; I will tell of all your wonderful deeds. I will be glad and rejoice in you; I will sing the praises of your name, O Most High. PSALM 9:1–2

Lord our God, keep us in your Spirit. Surround us with your protection, so that in body and soul we may praise your might and be joyful even in a world full of evil. Shine into our hearts, that we may discern what is right and good and eternal. May you do more than we can ask or understand for those who still walk in darkness far away from you. May your eternal mercy enfold them, and may the earth be filled with thanks to you, the Creator and Father of us all. Amen.

6

February

I will be glad and rejoice in your love, for you saw my affliction and knew the anguish of my soul. PSALM 31:7

Dear Father in heaven, we come before your presence with thanksgiving and rejoice that you are with us on earth. Even though we have many struggles and temptations and even though problems crowd in upon us, we know that we are in your hands and that everything must go according to your will. Hold us securely in your hand. Help us to bear all that we find hard, for we know you are in control and you lead everything to a good end. The darker and more difficult it may seem, the more clearly your hand will reveal the victory in those whose lives are founded in eternity, whose lives cannot end in sorrow but will end in your glory. Amen.

7

February

But one thing I do: Forgetting what is behind and straining toward what is ahead, I press on toward the goal to win the prize for which God has called me heavenward in Christ Jesus. PHILIPPIANS 3:13B–14

Dear Father in heaven, living source of all that is eternal in us, we come to you and plead with you to strengthen the gifts you have given us. Grant us the light of life in which we can walk in spite of the many burdens and uncertainties of our earthly life. Protect us from deception and disappointment. Strengthen our hope for your steadfast, firm, and eternal rule in us, in many others, and finally in all people. Amen.

8

February

For those who are led by the Spirit of God are the children of God. The Spirit you received does not make you slaves, so that you live in fear again; rather, the Spirit you received brought about your adoption to sonship. And by him we cry, "Abba, Father." The Spirit himself testifies with our spirit that we are God's children.

ROMANS 8:14–16

Dear Father in heaven, you are among us and we can call you Abba, dear Father. In the joy of being your children we want to lay our lives into your hands to be made good and happy. Care for us like a shepherd pasturing his flock so that we can have community with one another. Help us to realize that you have many children here and everywhere, and that again and again you take a child by the hand saying, "You are mine. I am caring for you." We thank you that your eyes watch over all the world. We thank you that your rule is over all humankind and will bring good to all people, wherever they may live. May this happen soon through our Savior. We call to him, "Lord Jesus, come. Come soon! May your hand keep us all close to the Father in heaven." Amen.

9

February

Whoever dwells in the shelter of the Most High will rest in the shadow of the Almighty. I will say of the Lord, "He is my refuge and my fortress, my God, in whom I trust." PSALM 91:1–2

Lord our God, we come into your presence, for you are our certainty, our refuge, especially in these times when so much is happening to grieve and trouble us. You are our God and our Savior today and for all time. You have always been our Savior and helper, and you will remain our Savior and helper forever. We praise you and glorify your name. Give a new spirit in our day, we pray, new help through the gospel brought by Jesus Christ. May your name be kept holy, your kingdom come, and your will be done on earth as in heaven. Amen.

10
February

In that day this song will be sung in the land of Judah: We have a strong city; God makes salvation its walls and ramparts. . . . Trust in the Lord forever, for the Lord, the Lord himself, is the Rock eternal. ISAIAH 26:1, 4

Lord our God, help us find the path that we may walk with confidence because you are our Father. Banish all thoughts that try to depress us. Let your Spirit drive them away. May our hearts become quiet before you, because you, the Almighty, guide everything for the good of people on earth. Everything will lead to thanksgiving, to your praise and glory. Be with us at all times, day and night. May our hearts always exult afresh, rejoicing in you, our God and our Savior. Amen.

11

February

But when he, the Spirit of truth, comes, he will guide you into all the truth. He will not speak on his own; he will speak only what he hears, and he will tell you what is yet to come. JOHN 16:13

Dear Father in heaven, grant your Spirit to us, your children. May something from you be revealed on earth so that divine strength and divine truth, not what is only human, are with us in all we do. Keep courage alive in our hearts even when things look dark. May powers of peace and healing be revealed through us because you are near and your kingdom is all around us. You can do all things, also things beyond our understanding. With your help we do what we are able, but we cannot do what you do. We trust in you, and we believe that through your power and your Spirit you will take possession of our whole lives and the lives of the many who sigh in their hearts for absolute truth. Amen.

12

February

However, do not rejoice that the spirits submit to you, but rejoice that your names are written in heaven.

LUKE 10:20

Dear Father in heaven, we thank you with all our hearts for showing your power in us and for overcoming so much that is hostile and that threatens to harm our life. We thank you for the countless wonders you do for our sake. We rejoice and thank you most of all for allowing us to know that you are writing our names in heaven. Where our names are, there we are too. Where our Lord Jesus Christ is, there we want to be too, and our words and our actions should come from him. Keep us faithful in this, and let us serve you with gladness on every path we tread. Amen.

13

February

Accept whatever befalls you, and in times of humiliation be patient. For gold is tested in the fire, and those found acceptable, in the furnace of humiliation.

ECCLESIASTICUS 2:4–5, NRSV

Lord our God, we thank you for helping us again and again. Praised be your name for all you do for us and for all your help in many dangers and hardships! We trust you completely and have faith in you through Jesus Christ, the Savior. He reveals your grace everywhere, in every hardship, giving us the courage and freedom to look toward your kingdom. Help us remain courageous when we have to face suffering, for we want to be your disciples in Jesus Christ, the Crucified One. He has made suffering holy, that our suffering too may bear fruit for you in time and in eternity. Amen.

14

February

Therefore, since we have been justified through faith, we have peace with God through our Lord Jesus Christ, through whom we have gained access by faith into this grace in which we now stand. And we boast in the hope of the glory of God. Not only so, but we also glory in our sufferings, because we know that suffering produces perseverance; perseverance, character; and character, hope. And hope does not put us to shame, because God's love has been poured out into our hearts through the Holy Spirit, who has been given to us. ROMANS 5:1–5

Lord our God, keep us in the grace that is ours through Jesus Christ. Uphold others also in this grace. Reveal yourself everywhere to those who trust in you and who await your kingdom. May your blessing be on our household. We thank you for helping us, and with your help we want to be faithful to you. Then when hardships come, we can be certain of your presence. We know and trust you. We know and trust the Savior, and we know and trust the Holy Spirit, in whom we can have community and be strengthened to serve your glory. Amen.

15

February

For this is what the high and exalted One says – he who lives forever, whose name is holy: "I live in a high and holy place, but also with the one who is contrite and lowly in spirit, to revive the spirit of the lowly and to revive the heart of the contrite. ISAIAH 57:15

Dear Father in heaven, we thank you that even in need and misery we may feel and know that you are with the weak, for you are mighty in helping your children. You give the weak strength to serve you in spite of all their faults and weaknesses. Make us glad at heart for everything we are allowed to do and experience, because it serves you, your glory, and your kingdom until the day when others also are given eyes to see. Amen.

16

February

We have not received the spirit of the world but the Spirit who is from God, that we may understand what God has freely given us. 1 CORINTHIANS 2:12

Dear Father in heaven, open the door for us, we pray. Grant that we may come to you in spirit. Grant that in you we may find peace and courage for our whole lives. Lead us always by your Spirit. Help us to find your will on earth and grant us access to your heavenly powers, for alone we can do nothing. Strengthen our faith so that we can always serve you. Bless your Word in us. May our hearts be opened, for we are your children, O Lord our God, through Jesus Christ our Savior. Amen.

17
February

Sing to the Lord a new song, for he has done marvelous things; his right hand and his holy arm have worked salvation for him. The Lord has made his salvation known and revealed his righteousness to the nations. He has remembered his love and his faithfulness to Israel; all the ends of the earth have seen the salvation of our God.

PSALM 98:1–3

Lord our God, we thank you from our hearts, from the bottom of our hearts, that you consider us worthy to work with you so that redemption may come to the world in Jesus Christ. Already today many are rejoicing in their Redeemer. They are full of hope and comfort because the end is approaching – that evening when your glory shall be revealed, when the whole world and all nations shall glorify you, O great God and Father in heaven. Come into our time, we pray. Help us, Lord our God. Day and night we look to you in the hope of beholding the time of your glory, in the hope of receiving the peace that is beyond all understanding and of finding redemption, the great redemption from heaven, through you, the God over all flesh. Amen.

18

February

He gives strength to the weary and increases the power of the weak. Even youths grow tired and weary, and young men stumble and fall; but those who hope in the Lord will renew their strength. They will soar on wings like eagles; they will run and not grow weary, they will walk and not be faint. ISAIAH 40:29–31

Lord our God, our loving Father, we thank you for all that our hearts and spirits are allowed to receive from you. We thank you for the community you give us, strengthening us to face life even through toil, struggle, and privation. Grant that your powers flow out to give us strength and courage. May we see and recognize you in your deeds ever more clearly. Do not let us faint or grow weary, no matter what we have to suffer. Grant that your Spirit may penetrate us ever more deeply to bring peace to us and those around us, and finally to bring blessing for all peoples of the earth. Amen.

19

February

And so we know and rely on the love God has for us. God is love. Whoever lives in love lives in God, and God in them. 1 JOHN 4:16

Lord our God, we come to you as poor, heavily burdened people who often do not know where to turn. But we have trust in you, for you are love. Your love penetrates deep into our lives, righting what is wrong and making amends for our blundering. And so we are joyful and await your grace and your help on all our ways. Bless us, and help us find what is right in every situation, to your praise and your honor. Amen.

20

February

My son, do not despise the Lord's discipline, and do not resent his rebuke, because the Lord disciplines those he loves, as a father the son he delights in. PROVERBS 3:11–12

Lord our God, we thank you that in spite of all the evil, we may look toward the good and toward a change for the better. For your love, your Spirit of love, can be with us. In spite of all that has gone wrong, we can change. Through genuine faith we can become worthy in your sight. Everything can turn to the good. The nations can become glad, rejoicing in life because you are working among them to help them change. Amen.

21
February

Husbands, love your wives, just as Christ loved the church and gave himself up for her to make her holy, cleansing her by the washing with water through the word, and to present her to himself as a radiant church, without stain or wrinkle or any other blemish, but holy and blameless.

EPHESIANS 5:25–27

Lord our God, remember us even though we are only a few. Protect us from all evil, from all inner harm, which threatens us every day. Let your hand be over us so that at last a great power may stream out from your church into all the world, bringing the fulfillment of your promises. We thank you for all your goodness. Watch over us, we pray. Keep us in the right spirit and purpose, and help us resist all that is wrong and harmful. Grant that we serve you and not the world. Protect us this day and every day. Amen.

22

February

And he passed in front of Moses, proclaiming, "The Lord, the Lord, the compassionate and gracious God, slow to anger, abounding in love and faithfulness, maintaining love to thousands, and forgiving wickedness, rebellion and sin. Yet he does not leave the guilty unpunished; he punishes the children and their children for the sin of the parents to the third and fourth generation."

EXODUS 34:6–7

Dear Father in heaven, how great are your goodness and mercy to us all on earth, who are subject to misery and death! May our hearts be strengthened through your goodness and through the saving power of your nature, revealed to us in Jesus Christ, our Redeemer. Protect and bless us this night. May your Spirit help us find your ever-present kindness and mercy. Praised be your name forever! Amen.

23

February

After this I looked, and there before me was a great multitude that no one could number, from every nation, from all tribes and peoples and tongues, standing before the throne and before the Lamb. They were clothed in white robes, with palm branches in their hands. And they cried out with a loud voice, "Salvation belongs to our God who sits on the throne, and to the Lamb!"

REVELATION 7:9–10

Lord God, we turn to you, praying that your kingdom may come. May your Jerusalem really come on earth, with all those blessed ones who are allowed to gather around Jesus Christ through forgiveness of sins and the resurrection. Come with your light into our time so that sins may be forgiven and people may find salvation. Remember those in great distress. Come with your help to those struggling with sin or death, for help can come from you alone. Nothing can help us except your fatherly love in Jesus Christ. Praised be your name! Amen.

24

February

For I am the Lord your God, who stirs up the sea so that its waves roar – the Lord Almighty is his name. I have put my words in your mouth and covered you with the shadow of my hand – I who set the heavens in place, who laid the foundations of the earth, and who say to Zion, "You are my people." ISAIAH 51:15–16

Lord God Almighty, your eyes watch over the whole world. We come before you with the evils that surround us still clinging to us. Shelter our lives in your hands. Give us your strength to win through, even in suffering and need. For we are yours, O Lord our God. You have chosen your people to strengthen them and to free them from all evil. We beseech you to help us. May we feel your presence among us. May your Word bear fruit in us to the everlasting honor of your name. Amen.

25

February

Here is my servant, whom I uphold, my chosen one in whom I delight; I will put my Spirit on him, and he will bring justice to the nations. ISAIAH 42:1

Dear Father in heaven, grant that we may stand in your grace. Grant that the light of your grace may come to us through your Word. Keep us firm in faith until the promised time when your redemption shall come to all the nations on earth. We are often anxious and ask ourselves if people can bear it. Will they learn to listen to your Word? Will they remain steadfast when hard times come? Will they turn to you alone, to you who know the hour and appoint the time when we may see the promised day? Let the might of your hand prevail over the whole world. You are the only power that can help us out of our great affliction, you our only Lord. Amen.

26

February

I lift up my eyes to the mountains – where does my help come from? My help comes from the Lord, the Maker of heaven and earth. PSALM 121:1–2

Lord our God, our refuge for ever and ever, bless us as we gather in your presence and turn to you. May we be your children, who can simply believe and stand firm in our lives and in our calling. We thank you for giving us your grace and constant help. In your grace we can be joyful, praising and honoring you. You are our Father. You never forsake us. May your name be praised by us all. May your name be praised above and in the whole world so that all people may acknowledge you and receive what they need from you. Amen.

27
February

Do not be afraid of what you are about to suffer. I tell you, the devil will put some of you in prison to test you, and you will suffer persecution for ten days. Be faithful, even to the point of death, and I will give you life as your victor's crown. REVELATION 2:10

Lord our God, we come into your presence. Hear our prayers, we entreat you. Let your will be done among us; let your will be done for each one of us individually, and for our time. Let everything go according to your will, even if the way leads through tribulation, fear, and need. For in the end your goal will be reached. In the end you will fulfill your purpose, and your kingdom will come. Your kingdom will come to the honor of your name and for the redemption of all people still suffering on earth. Let your Word bring us blessing. May we go forward joyfully in the patience of Jesus Christ until times change, until a new day dawns and we are allowed to see your glory and your peace. Amen.

28
February

For great is your love, reaching to the heavens; your faithfulness reaches to the skies. Be exalted, O God, above the heavens; let your glory be over all the earth.

PSALM 57:10–11

Dear Father in heaven, we thank you that you have always been gracious to us, revealing your great goodness and power in ages past and in the present. In this revelation we live, O Lord our God. You are the almighty One, who works wonders on earth and who rules the heavens so that we can be blest and helped on our earthly paths. Let your goodness and your justice be revealed throughout all the world. Arise, O Lord our God. Let your light shine in us who believe in you. Let your light shine into the whole world. Let your name be glorified. You are indeed our Father, both in heaven and on earth. You give our lives security now and in eternity. Amen.

29
February

For the word of God is alive and active. Sharper than any double-edged sword, it penetrates even to dividing soul and spirit, joints and marrow; it judges the thoughts and attitudes of the heart. HEBREWS 4:12

Lord our God, be merciful to us. Be our strong refuge. Help us on all our ways. Help us on the dark and difficult paths we must often travel on earth. Grant that we may see your light, for you are with us. You help us, and you let the power of the life of Jesus Christ be with us so that your name is honored on earth through many who love you and come to you, pleading with you in prayer. Give us the light of your Word, that we may hear and live rightly. Give us increasing strength for the fight to which you have called us. Bless us all. Shine into our hearts so that we can carry out all you have promised through your Word. Amen.

March

I

March

Taste and see that the Lord is good; blessed is the one who takes refuge in him. PSALM 34:8

Dear Father in heaven, we come to you. With thanks we come to you, for again and again you have helped us. Again and again you have let your light shine out on us so that we could be glad and know that our lives are in your hands. Protect us on this earth, where it is so necessary. Protect us, that the light of true life may shine more and more brightly and we may praise your name with our whole heart. Be with us this night, O God, and touch our hearts with your Spirit. Amen.

2

March

Dear friends, do not be surprised at the fiery ordeal that has come on you to test you, as though something strange were happening to you. But rejoice inasmuch as you participate in the sufferings of Christ, so that you may be overjoyed when his glory is revealed. I PETER 4:12–13

Dear Father in heaven, we ask you from our hearts to give us your peace. Grant that nothing may take your peace from us, and protect us from all that is evil. May we always be mindful that we should serve you in self-denial. May we be faithful on all our ways, looking to the great promise you have given each one of us. Keep us under your protection, as you have always done. We praise and thank you for all that comes to our hearts from you, making us full of trust and certain of your further help. Amen.

3
March

Then he said to them all: "Whoever wants to be my disciple must deny themselves and take up their cross daily and follow me. For whoever wants to save their life will lose it, but whoever loses their life for me will save it."

LUKE 9:23–24

Dear Father in heaven, you have sent us the Lord Jesus to bear our guilt and our misery. To this day we rejoice that he came, he who can free us from all evil. Teach us to understand the way of the Cross, the way Jesus went. Grant that we may always follow him, even if we also suffer and have a cross to bear. Then we can joyfully go the way he went to the glory of your name, O Father in heaven. We are your children whether we understand it or not. You protect and care for us, until your glory comes and everything is completed that was begun through Jesus Christ, the Savior of the world. Bless us in his Word, and help us to become his true followers. Amen.

4

March

Therefore, since we are surrounded by such a great cloud of witnesses, let us throw off everything that hinders and the sin that so easily entangles. And let us run with perseverance the race marked out for us, fixing our eyes on Jesus, the pioneer and perfecter of faith. For the joy set before him he endured the cross, scorning its shame, and sat down at the right hand of the throne of God.

HEBREWS 12:1–2

Lord, our God and Father, we thank you for letting us walk in the way of Jesus Christ, for helping us on the way to the Cross. Come what may, we belong to the Savior, and we are your children. We want to be joyful and full of faith, full of hope, full of patience, for your mercy leads us on. In all we experience how often we can say, "Thanks be to God. He has helped us here, he has helped there, he helps every day in spite of all the evil in the world. Praise and thanks and honor be to him forever!" Amen.

5

March

Do not be afraid, little flock, for your Father has been pleased to give you the kingdom. LUKE 12:32

Lord our God, we come to you as a little flock, asking you to accept us and keep us as your own, whom you will redeem in your time. Protect us always so that we remain strong in faith. Strengthen us in the faith that you are with us, helping us. Grant that your people may come to the light, to the honor of your name. So we entrust ourselves to your hands this night. Be with us, Lord our God, through your Spirit. Amen.

6

March

Ascribe to the Lord, all you families of nations, ascribe to the Lord glory and strength. Ascribe to the Lord the glory due his name; bring an offering and come into his courts. Worship the Lord in the splendor of his holiness; tremble before him, all the earth. PSALM 96:7–9

Lord our God, you are our help and our comfort. We look to you and to your promises. Grant that we may remain full of courage, also in our personal concerns, so that we do not complain like fretful children, but cheerfully wait for your great victory on earth. May we become your people. Grant your Spirit to your people, not only to a few but eventually to many. Lord our God, we pray that your will may be done on earth among the nations; may your will be done on earth as it is done in heaven. Amen.

7

March

The Lord is my strength and my defense; he has become my salvation. Shouts of joy and victory resound in the tents of the righteous: "The Lord's right hand has done mighty things! The Lord's right hand is lifted high; the Lord's right hand has done mighty things!"

PSALM 118:14–16

Dear Father in heaven, we are your children, and we look to you and to your help at every turn of our lives. Remember us, especially when we want to serve you. Stay with us with your Spirit so that everything may work out to further your kingdom and the victory of Jesus Christ, which is to be proclaimed on earth. Through his victory all people shall find in him their Savior and look to you, our Father in heaven. Yes, Father in heaven, have mercy on the world, on the many who are unfortunate and who suffer from the widespread evil around them. Remember them. Have mercy on us through the strong and mighty Lord, Jesus Christ. Amen.

8
March

Therefore God exalted him to the highest place and gave him the name that is above every name, that at the name of Jesus every knee should bow, in heaven and on earth and under the earth, and every tongue acknowledge that Jesus Christ is Lord, to the glory of God the Father.

PHILIPPIANS 2:9–11

Lord Jesus, we bow before you, before you to whom all power is given. We will love you, O Lord. We will treasure you. Your thoughts shall be our thoughts, that we may learn how you are named in heaven, on earth, and below the earth. Watch over us and be with us until you can come, until the time is fulfilled when you will appear among us and establish God's kingdom. Then the whole world will rejoice and all people will bend their knees before you, the one Lord and Savior. Amen.

9
March

But if we walk in the light, as he is in the light, we have fellowship with one another, and the blood of Jesus, his Son, purifies us from all sin. 1 JOHN 1:7

Dear Father in heaven, we thank you as your children, whom you know how to gather. You have brought us into community with you in a wonderful way, in the midst of a world full of unrest, full of misery, and full of sin. For you know your children and lead them into community with you. You comfort them. You give them strength of faith, and confidence in your rulership and your kingdom, which will prevail over everything evil and deathly that still seems to control humankind. But your dominion reaches far, far beyond. You will keep us in your hands. For the sake of those who trust in you, you will send your grace and your help into the whole world. Amen.

10

March

As the rain and the snow come down from heaven, and do not return to it without watering the earth and making it bud and flourish, so that it yields seed for the sower and bread for the eater, so is my word that goes out from my mouth: It will not return to me empty, but will accomplish what I desire and achieve the purpose for which I sent it. ISAIAH 55:10–11

Lord our God, light of the world and light of our human life, we thank you for sending your Word into our hearts. Your Word works within us and allows us to rejoice. Even if we often experience hard and bitter times here on earth, we can rejoice already, as the world shall rejoice when your will and your Word are fulfilled. Protect us, and keep us pure and free in spirit, that we may be your servants, that we may sometimes be allowed to say a little word in harmony with the great, powerful Word which you have sent into the world. Amen.

11

March

Therefore, since we have been justified through faith, we have peace with God through our Lord Jesus Christ, through whom we have gained access by faith into this grace in which we now stand. And we boast in the hope of the glory of God. ROMANS 5:1–2

Dear Father in heaven, grant that we may share in the community of your Holy Spirit. In community with you our earthly troubles fall away and we remain in your peace in spite of all our failures and shortcomings, in spite of all the toil we must gladly take upon ourselves. Watch over us. Keep our hearts unshaken, clear, and steady. Keep us in the certainty that your kingdom is coming, is already beginning and can be plainly seen, so that all people can receive the good you have planned for them. Be with us this night. Amen.

12
March

But now, this is what the Lord says – he who created you, Jacob, he who formed you, Israel: "Do not fear, for I have redeemed you; I have summoned you by name; you are mine. When you pass through the waters, I will be with you; and when you pass through the rivers, they will not sweep over you. When you walk through the fire, you will not be burned; the flames will not set you ablaze."

ISAIAH 43:1–2

Dear Father in heaven, we thank you for the gift of your light in our hearts, allowing us to have faith in you. We thank you for your light, which shows us the many ways you save us from need, darkness, and death. In the midst of this darkness you keep our hearts safe so that we can be faithful until your time comes, the time when you will reveal yourself to the world, and when all voices will cry out as one, "Yes, Father in heaven, we thank you. You have redeemed us all." Amen.

13

March

Blessed are those who hunger and thirst for righteousness, for they will be filled. MATTHEW 5:6

Dear Father in heaven, may our hearts find words to praise you together, to ask you with one accord that we may be brought into community with you. We come to you with our whole selves, with all that we have experienced, with all that has been given to us through your leading. For to this day you have shown us the way, guiding us through right and wrong, through the perfect and the imperfect. You have led us all to know that we belong to you. We are yours. You are working in us to bring about what you have in mind for each one of us and for the many, many who hunger and thirst for justice and truth. Be with us through your Spirit. Touch us through the hand of Jesus Christ. He is our Savior, and we hold fast to him so that we can praise you in his name. Amen.

14

March

Then the Lord will create over all of Mount Zion and over those who assemble there a cloud of smoke by day and a glow of flaming fire by night; over everything the glory will be a canopy. It will be a shelter and shade from the heat of the day, and a refuge and hiding place from the storm and rain. ISAIAH 4:5–6

Dear Father in heaven, our refuge for this day and for each day to come, touch us with the finger of your power. Be our protection and strong defense against all attacks of darkness. Where people look to you out of the darkness, let their eyes grow shining bright with the light from your eyes. Let your light shine within us and around us. Let your light bring your cause to victory, to the final great day of Jesus Christ. Amen.

15

March

Now may the God of peace, who through the blood of the eternal covenant brought back from the dead our Lord Jesus, that great Shepherd of the sheep, equip you with everything good for doing his will, and may he work in us what is pleasing to him, through Jesus Christ, to whom be glory for ever and ever. Amen. HEBREWS 13:20–21

Lord our God, through the Spirit grant us community with you, we pray. Help us onward again and again, and help us grow in strength to follow what is true and good. May your goodness and your grace be in our hearts to help us in all practical things. Grant that wherever we live we may have something of the power in which Jesus Christ lived and suffered, in which he died and yet lives again. May the world still learn that it has a redeemer and that it belongs to him, to the glory of your name. Amen.

16
March

Therefore I will give him a portion among the great, and he will divide the spoils with the strong, because he poured out his life unto death, and was numbered with the transgressors. For he bore the sin of many, and made intercession for the transgressors. ISAIAH 53:12

Dear Father in heaven, may we receive your Spirit so that we win the victory over ourselves and over the world around us, not with our human crudeness, force, and clamor, but only through your Spirit in the name of Jesus Christ. Help each of us in our own particular situation. We all know there is much evil around us; there is much we must fight. But in Jesus' name we want to plunge right in, right into the world, right into whatever suffering is meant for us in the midst of the evil that is not yet overcome. In Jesus' name we go toward the great victory that will come when all who are granted your joy will praise you with all their hearts, O Father in heaven. Amen.

17

March

To the Jews who had believed him, Jesus said, "If you hold to my teaching, you are really my disciples. Then you will know the truth, and the truth will set you free."

JOHN 8:31–32

Dear Father in heaven, grant that we may come to you in the Spirit. Through your Spirit gather us and many others on earth around our Lord Jesus Christ, the great Savior of humankind. May our hearts become truly free because you deliver us from all bondage to our own natures and to the world around us. As free people may we be led safely through distress, fear, and want, through need and death. May we become happy children whom Jesus Christ has called to life, children who are not discouraged by the struggle but who fight joyfully for your kingdom until it can be revealed to all the world. Amen.

18
March

May you be made strong with all the strength that comes from his glorious power, and may you be prepared to endure everything with patience, while joyfully giving thanks to the Father, who has enabled you to share in the inheritance of the saints in the light. He has rescued us from the power of darkness and transferred us into the kingdom of his beloved Son, in whom we have redemption, the forgiveness of sins. COLOSSIANS 1:11–14, NRSV

Dear Father in heaven, we thank you. We want to be ready to thank you at all times. We look forward with joy to your kingdom and await the redemption that will free us to the very depth of our being, to the praise and thanks and honor of your name. Be with the many people who come hungering and thirsting to you. Bring deliverance to those whose hearts are true, and let them know that the power of your kingdom is truly present here on earth in Jesus Christ, our Lord. Amen.

19

March

And in the very place where it was said to them, "You are not my people," there they will be called "children of the living God." ROMANS 9:26

Lord our God, we thank you that you have called us your children, a people who may serve you even in suffering and temptation. Grant that the grace of Jesus Christ may be in us so that we can be victorious over everything that life puts in our way and can withstand the distress that surrounds so many people. O Lord our God, our only refuge, to you alone can we appeal for evil to end and for the victory of Jesus Christ to break through. In that hour we shall rejoice and be glad as your people. Amen.

20

March

Then I heard a loud voice in heaven say: "Now have come the salvation and the power and the kingdom of our God, and the authority of his Messiah. For the accuser of our brothers and sisters…has been hurled down. They triumphed over him by the blood of the Lamb and by the word of their testimony; they did not love their lives so much as to shrink from death. REVELATION 12:10–11

Lord our God, in praise and thanksgiving we look toward your kingdom and the reign of Jesus Christ in your kingdom. We rejoice that you make him Lord not only in heaven but also on earth, where he will gain the victory in all humankind. We will become good and will love one another, and will find peace when everything is done according to your will. For the time must come when, on earth as in heaven, your will is done everywhere and in everything. Be with us with your Spirit so that we may stand firm as your children until the moment comes for us to exult: Up out of all grief and trouble! Up from evil and death! Up to you, our Father in heaven! Praise to your name. Glory to Jesus Christ our Savior, whom you have given us. Amen.

21

March

Till the Spirit is poured on us from on high, and the desert becomes a fertile field, and the fertile field seems like a forest. The Lord's justice will dwell in the desert, his righteousness live in the fertile field. The fruit of that righteousness will be peace; its effect will be quietness and confidence forever. ISAIAH 32:15–17

Lord our God, we look to your Holy Spirit. Unite us with your Spirit, we pray. May we be children of your Spirit, ruled throughout our lives by your Spirit. There is so much else around us wanting to teach us and claiming to represent the truth, and we are full of fear unless help comes from your Spirit alone. Your Spirit comes to us as helper and comforter, who helps us find the way to go. Hear us, your children, whom you want to lead and whose Savior you want to be through Jesus Christ, our Lord. Amen.

22
March

He destined us for adoption as his children through Jesus Christ, according to the good pleasure of his will, to the praise of his glorious grace that he freely bestowed on us in the Beloved. EPHESIANS 1:5–6, NRSV

Dear Father in heaven, grant that we may come to you as your children. Grant that we may come to your Spirit, that something of trust and perseverance may be born in us for our life on earth. May we always be loyal and full of hope, working and striving not only for what is earthly, but for the tasks that have been laid on us for your kingdom and its righteousness. Let new light shine out among us again and again. Let many understand when your voice is speaking to them, so that they may gain courage. Let your voice be heard so that the great gospel that makes us your children may be proclaimed to people of all circles. Amen.

23

March

This is what the Lord says: "In the time of my favor I will answer you, and in the day of salvation I will help you; I will keep you and will make you to be a covenant for the people, to restore the land and to reassign its desolate inheritances." ISAIAH 49:8

Lord our God, protect us in your Spirit. Strengthen our hearts especially when we often have to bear suffering, that we may be steadfast in hope and may again and again experience a day of salvation. Protect us in every way. Accept our praise and thanks, and let our hearts rejoice in what you have already done for us. We want to discern your ways more and more so that we may please you as your servants. Amen.

24
March

For the revelation awaits an appointed time; it speaks of the end and will not prove false. Though it linger, wait for it; it will certainly come and will not delay.

HABAKKUK 2:3

Dear Father in heaven, in quietness we come to you and ask you for your Spirit. We ask this especially for the time of waiting still required of us as we hope and strive for light to come into all hearts, for light to shine where there is so much death. We must not despair of our inner life even when life around us rages as if it would suck us down into its whirlpool with no way out. But you will guard us. Watch over us, we pray, also in hours of temptation, so that we may remain under your care. Watch over us so that we have hope and joy in you, assured that your goal for us all is true life from above, a life of resurrection. Amen.

25
March

As a father has compassion on his children, so the Lord has compassion on those who fear him; for he knows how we are formed, he remembers that we are dust.

PSALM 103:13–14

Lord our God, merciful God and almighty Father in heaven, we beseech you, look upon us as your children. For in spite of everything, all of us are allowed to be your children and to praise you for all the good you are doing and for all you still want to do for us. Hear our prayer as we come to you with particular concerns, asking for your will to be done in us, for everything to be carried out according to your good purpose, that we may be joyful even in hard and serious times and may hold fast to what you have promised. Amen.

26

March

The Lord is not slow in keeping his promise, as some understand slowness. Instead he is patient with you, not wanting anyone to perish, but everyone to come to repentance. 2 PETER 3:9

Dear Father in heaven, we thank you with all our hearts that you have given us your living promise. We thank you that again and again our faith can receive a clearer vision through this promise. For you have promised that at last the greatest day of all will come, will conquer the whole world, and bring salvation to all people to the glory of your name as Father throughout all nations. Strengthen us in every way, especially when we are in need and distress. Strengthen the sick and those who are tempted. May they wait in expectation for fulfillment of the promise, and may they see help come. May your name, Lord God, be honored among us. May your kingdom come and your will be done on earth as in heaven. Amen.

27
March

For no matter how many promises God has made, they are "Yes" in Christ. And so through him the "Amen" is spoken by us to the glory of God. Now it is God who makes both us and you stand firm in Christ. He anointed us, set his seal of ownership on us, and put his Spirit in our hearts as a deposit, guaranteeing what is to come.

2 CORINTHIANS 1:20–22

Lord our God, from whom great promises are given for all humankind and especially for your people, we gather in your presence. We rejoice before you, for your promise is sure and your works will be revealed to the glory of your name. Grant us steadfast faith in the grace of Jesus Christ. Grant us faith to hold firm, and in spite of all evil to trust that you are ruling and will set everything right. Lord our God, our Father, we cry to you. As the deer pants for refreshing water, so in our time our souls cry out to you, "Our Father in heaven, may your name be honored. May your kingdom come. May your will be done on earth as in heaven." Amen.

28

March

My dear children, I write this to you so that you will not sin. But if anybody does sin, we have an advocate with the Father – Jesus Christ, the Righteous One. He is the atoning sacrifice for our sins, and not only for ours but also for the sins of the whole world. 1 JOHN 2:1–2

Lord God, we thank you that you have given us atonement, an atonement that delivers us from all evil, from all that is temporal and perishable, and that allows us even now to live in eternity. Grant that many people become aware of the greatness and freeing power of the redemption you have offered us. May a people be born to you, serving you with light in their hearts as they look to the future coming of Jesus Christ. Be with us, strengthen us, and protect us from all the deception on earth. For we want to be your children and nothing else; with our whole hearts we want to look always to you. Amen.

29
March

"Because he loves me," says the Lord, "I will rescue him; I will protect him, for he acknowledges my name. He will call on me, and I will answer him; I will be with him in trouble, I will deliver him and honor him. With long life I will satisfy him and show him my salvation."

PSALM 91:14–16

Lord our God, dear Father in heaven, we turn our hearts to you, for you know all our need. We turn to you, for you are ready with your help when we are at our wit's end. You have paths we can follow joyfully because we have a Lord who rules and who reigns over us to make us glad. May we praise your name at all times. May your help be always before our eyes so that we can be your true children, to the glory of your name on earth. Amen.

30

March

We wait in hope for the Lord; he is our help and our shield. In him our hearts rejoice, for we trust in his holy name. May your unfailing love be with us, Lord, even as we put our hope in you. PSALM 33:20–22

Lord God, we thank you for having revealed yourself on this earth in the midst of sin, need, and oppression. We thank you that we can have joy in all you have done both before and since the coming of Jesus Christ, our Savior in everything. To you be praise and thanks. Our hearts leap up with joy in you and in your deeds. Grant that we may be faithful to the end, victorious in all things through your Spirit, who helps and blesses us on our way. Grant your help to all who call to you and who long to rejoice in you. Amen.

31
March

We know also that the Son of God has come and has given us understanding, so that we may know him who is true. And we are in him who is true by being in his Son Jesus Christ. He is the true God and eternal life.

I JOHN 5:20

Lord our God, we turn our faces to you and plead with you to come to us earthly and often tormented people. May we find strength in the Lord Jesus Christ, through whom redemption is promised to us all. May your kingdom at last be revealed and everything change for the better even though we do not see it yet. May we always honor your name above all others, for you are our Father and we hold fast to your grace that lets us call you Father. In our troubled times grant us enduring faith that you can bring a new time when good shall at last emerge from all the distress. Grant that every broken and needy person may experience your help, your grace, and your salvation, and may know that these always surround us, if only our eyes are open to see and recognize them. We thank and praise you at all times. Amen.

April

I

April

For the Lord is good and his love endures forever; his faithfulness continues through all generations.

PSALM 100:5

Lord God, our Father, we thank you for all the light you give us and for all your loving help in outward things as well. We come into your presence and ask you to give us your light and your constant guidance for the path we must follow. Grant that what is of heaven may be revealed on earth, that we may rejoice in the good and beautiful things you give to all people. Our Father, reveal what is of heaven, and free people from their sin and darkness so that at last they recognize your glory. Strengthen our hope for this goal. Rule and work in the hearts of many people, that through them your glory may be proclaimed to all. Amen.

2

April

Lift up your eyes to the heavens, look at the earth beneath; the heavens will vanish like smoke, the earth will wear out like a garment and its inhabitants die like flies. But my salvation will last forever, my righteousness will never fail. ISAIAH 51:6

Lord our God, in you we want to find our strength, in you we want to hold out even in these times. We rejoice that the end is coming, the end you are preparing, when your salvation and justice will come on earth according to your promises. Be with us and with the believing circle given to us through Jesus Christ. Make us alert and give us fresh courage again and again, however difficult life may be. We want to continue to live and find strength in the grace of Jesus Christ, holding on in joy without grumbling and complaining. Lord God, may your name be honored, your kingdom come, and your will be done in us according to your plan. Amen.

3

April

In the last days the mountain of the Lord's temple will be established as the highest of the mountains; it will be exalted above the hills, and all nations will stream to it. Many peoples will come and say, "Come, let us go up to the mountain of the Lord, to the temple of the God of Jacob. He will teach us his ways, so that we may walk in his paths." ISAIAH 2:2–3A

Dear Father in heaven, we thank you that we have you and the light of your Spirit, which always gives us new determination for the tasks you ask of us. We thank you that we may live not just in the passing moment but also in eternity, looking with joyful hope to the future meant for us and for all humankind. Keep us in your Spirit, and open to us truth after truth. May we be part of that people who carry a light within them, a light which will show them the way through all the struggles and temptations of life; then each one of us will know day by day that you can help us and everyone on earth to a better life through your Holy Spirit. Amen.

4
April

John gave this testimony: "I saw the Spirit come down from heaven as a dove and remain on him…I have seen and I testify that this is God's Chosen One."

JOHN 1:32, 34

Our Father in heaven, as your children may we truly receive something from you to bring our lives into a living bond with you. Grant that we may overcome everything harmful and evil. May it be given to us to help that your kingdom may come closer and closer, that your will may be done, and Jesus Christ, your Son, may be recognized as the light of the world for the salvation of all people and their deliverance from all evil. Protect us and grant that your Spirit may remain with us. Amen.

5
April

Yes, my soul, find rest in God; my hope comes from him. Truly he is my rock and my salvation; he is my fortress, I will not be shaken. My salvation and my honor depend on God; he is my mighty rock, my refuge. Trust in him at all times, you people; pour out your hearts to him, for God is our refuge. PSALM 62:5–8

Dear Father in heaven, we thank you for this day and for all the loving kindness you pour out on us. May we continue to receive your help and your protection. Bless us in whatever we are allowed to do in your service, that it may always be done in love to all people. Watch over us this night and be with us. May your will be done throughout the world, so that at last all confusion may come to an end, Satan's work may be destroyed, and your children may shout for joy that your will is being done on earth as in heaven. Amen.

6
April

For I resolved to know nothing while I was with you except Jesus Christ and him crucified.

I CORINTHIANS 2:2

Lord our God, Father of us all, bless our community in the name of our Savior Jesus Christ. May your Spirit carry out what we are powerless to do, so that we experience strength and joy, something from eternity, and can face life with all its evil, pain, and suffering. For you have drawn us to yourself, and in spirit, soul, and body we belong to another world, higher than this earthly and passing one. We want to remain true to this higher world, that your praise may come from one heart and from one voice, that the name of Jesus Christ may shine in us and show us the way to all that is true and eternal. Amen.

7

April

And I will ask the Father, and he will give you another advocate to help you and be with you forever – the Spirit of truth. The world cannot accept him, because it neither sees him nor knows him. But you know him, for he lives with you and will be in you. JOHN 14:16-17

Lord our God and our Father, we thank you for giving us the Holy Spirit, who binds us to you. Give us continually afresh something of this Spirit so that we can go forward with light shining on the paths we must follow on earth. Grant us your Spirit, grant that light may break into our whole life and we can rejoice because we experience so much of what you are doing. For through the power of your Spirit you can help us toward your future and all that is to come, that we may live not only in time but in eternity. Amen.

8

April

He replied, "Because you have so little faith. Truly I tell you, if you have faith as small as a mustard seed, you can say to this mountain, 'Move from here to there,' and it will move. Nothing will be impossible for you."

MATTHEW 17:20

Lord our God, we thank you for revealing your rulership, which is for the good of each of us. Each one of us will become what we ought to be when our faith is united with your divine power. Protect this faith in us through every temptation and through all we have yet to endure in this earthly life. Free us again and again for one thing alone, that your kingdom may come into being within us and around us, to the praise and glory of the everlasting truth you have given us in Jesus Christ. Amen.

9

April

I will not leave you as orphans; I will come to you. Before long, the world will not see me anymore, but you will see me. Because I live, you also will live. On that day you will realize that I am in my Father, and you are in me, and I am in you. Whoever has my commands and keeps them is the one who loves me. The one who loves me will be loved by my Father, and I too will love them and show myself to them." JOHN 14:16-17

Lord our God, dear Father in heaven, we are gathered in your presence through Jesus Christ, our Lord. Reveal to us our Savior Jesus Christ. May the Savior be revealed to us; otherwise in our need we will never come through. Grant that at this late hour for the world we may see him as he is, and through him and through the kingdom that he brings we may be lifted above the troubles of our time. Strengthen our hearts every day, and fill us with joy because you guide everything on earth as in heaven; in the end you will give us the victory that belongs to the kingdom you have founded. May we be comforted through all eternity in this kingdom, a kingdom far greater and more glorious than all the kingdoms of the world. Amen.

10
April

For none of us lives for ourselves alone, and none of us dies for ourselves alone. If we live, we live for the Lord; and if we die, we die for the Lord. So, whether we live or die, we belong to the Lord. For this very reason, Christ died and returned to life so that he might be the Lord of both the dead and the living. ROMANS 14:7–9

Lord God, unite us with Jesus Christ, the risen and living One. Unite us so that our lives are completely submerged in your will through Jesus Christ. Tear us loose from all that tries to bind us to earth. Make us free people who always lift their heads and look up because their redemption is approaching. Almighty God, we trust in you, however difficult the times may be. Remember all peoples, for it is your will to gather them into your kingdom. You, O God, are our refuge and our help. In you we trust until the end. Amen.

11

April

Whoever serves me must follow me; and where I am, my servant also will be. My Father will honor the one who serves me. JOHN 12:26

Dear Father in heaven, we thank you for this day and for the protection you have given us. Grant that we may find our joy in your grace and in your love. Help us to become truer followers of Jesus, who came in your love. Be merciful to us and help all those who belong to you. You know them all and the thoughts of their hearts. You know their struggle on earth and the temptations that surround them. Help each one, also those who are still far away from you. Give them hearts open to your Word and to all you have promised. We entrust ourselves to your care this night. Help us and bless us. May your will be done in all things, also in the midst of all the sin and misery in the world. May your will be done on earth as in heaven, and may your kingdom come. Amen.

12

April

But our citizenship is in heaven. And we eagerly await a Savior from there, the Lord Jesus Christ, who, by the power that enables him to bring everything under his control, will transform our lowly bodies so that they will be like his glorious body. PHILIPPIANS 3:20–21

Lord our God, draw us to yourself. Draw us into the quiet that you give, where something can happen to us and to our hearts. Help us to discern your kingdom surrounding us and in our spirits to live in this kingdom. Then our life will be as if in heaven, where we need not worry or torment ourselves, where your power is everything to us, penetrating our earthly life, which so often weighs us down. We thank you that you have made a way of strength, full of power to hold us firmly, so that even when we stumble, we cannot be turned from the goal. We thank you for all the good that comes from you, which we cannot see in earthly things but which can invade our hearts with such mighty and uplifting power. Amen.

13
April

Teach me to do your will, for you are my God; may your good Spirit lead me on level ground. PSALM 143:10

Lord our God, O great and almighty One, whose Spirit fills heaven and earth! We thank you that you are our Father and that in you we have a refuge wherever we must go as we serve you on earth. We thank you that your life can be revealed in us and can flow through us so that the world may be blest by you, our loving and caring Father. Protect us and strengthen us in times of trouble and sorrow. When we travel on new paths, give us your Spirit to show us the way, that everything may lead to the good and to your honor. Father, through your Spirit unite us in the unshakable hope that your will shall at last be done on earth as in heaven. Grant that we may rejoice in the certainty that whatever happens, our paths are made level and firm by your love and your faithfulness. Amen.

14

April

Jesus said to her, "I am the resurrection and the life. The one who believes in me will live, even though they die; and whoever lives by believing in me will never die. Do you believe this?" JOHN 11:25–26

Dear Father in heaven, to you we entrust everything, for you have given us life and will call us to resurrection. You will help your children, your people, to reach what you have called them to. Protect your Church on earth. Let her soon see your glory. Let her see Jesus Christ intervening in people's lives and destinies until, shaken and trembling, they have to recognize that they should love and honor Jesus alone, to your honor, O Father in heaven. We thank you for all you have given us in your Word, which enables us to become your children and to find your way for us on earth. Bless us and give us the Holy Spirit. Protect us this night. Protect us so that nothing evil can harm us. Amen.

15
April

But I trust in you, Lord; I say, "You are my God." My times are in your hands; deliver me from the hands of my enemies, from those who pursue me. Let your face shine on your servant; save me in your unfailing love.

PSALM 31:14–16

Dear Father in heaven, we turn to you. Hear our longing, hear our hopes, hear our faith! Our future lies in your hands. Free each heart from discouragement and sadness over the many evils of the world. Make us free from earthly things, free yet bound in spirit with you, O God. Help us on our pilgrimage toward eternity. As we walk with you, fill us with hope that the whole world will see the light, for in your light alone can we find fullness of life. Protect us and bless us through your Spirit. Amen.

16

April

Jesus answered, "I am the way and the truth and the life. No one comes to the Father except through me. If you really know me, you will know my Father as well. From now on, you do know him and have seen him."

JOHN 14:6–7

Lord our God, we come seeking to find community with you and ask you to keep us in your truth throughout all that occupies us in our daily lives. Keep us from growing confused about truths we have already found through the witness of your Spirit in our hearts. Keep us in your truth so that we can hold firmly to our course on earth under the many hardships and burdens that try to drag us down. Help us to remain steady and to find the path that goes straight ahead, leading us on and on to your final goal. Amen.

17

April

There remains, then, a Sabbath-rest for the people of God; for anyone who enters God's rest also rests from their works, just as God did from his. Let us, therefore, make every effort to enter that rest, so that no one will perish by following their example of disobedience.

HEBREWS 4:9–11

Dear Father in heaven, we thank you for everything you have done for us, everything we think of when we are quiet for a moment and look back. May all that you have done remain alive in us, so that we can look forward with open, clear-seeing eyes, aware that our lives are in your hands and that you always lead us to something new, great, and glorious. Again and again you will give your Sabbath rest to your people, to all who acknowledge you and whose task is to work for you among the people. Again and again you will bring them your rest, until the coming of the last and glorious Sabbath on which your kingdom can be established. Amen.

18
April

I know your deeds. See, I have placed before you an open door that no one can shut. I know that you have little strength, yet you have kept my word and have not denied my name. REVELATION 3:8

Dear Father in heaven, we thank you that you know us all and that you look deep into our hearts, watching over us in everything we go through, whether easy or difficult. We thank you that we do not stand alone but that you hear the smallest sigh of each of your children. We thank you that darkness must give way to light, distress to joy, and fear to strength and courage. For you lead us through everything; it is what you bring about from your future world, not anything within our sight, that gives us strength and courage and that endures through everything.

We thank you from our hearts for your unending gifts, and we are amazed that it was possible for us to receive all this from you. Protect us and keep us childlike, so that we remain in the fellowship that the Lord Jesus has given us, singing praise to him and to the glory and honor of your name. Amen.

19
April

Always giving thanks to God the Father for everything, in the name of our Lord Jesus Christ. EPHESIANS 5:20

Dear Father in heaven, accept our thanks today for all you allow us to learn and to receive from you. Help us, your children, to follow the Savior with a right spirit and with true understanding. Protect us from evil, from all the works of Satan. In our generation may we experience your rulership and your wonders. In the name of Jesus we pray, reveal yourself with power. May your will be done on earth as in heaven, that all may realize they are in your hands and that it is your will to set everything right. Be with us this night. Bless and strengthen us for all the work entrusted to us. Amen.

20

April

Before they call I will answer; while they are still speaking I will hear. ISAIAH 65:24

Our great God, still hidden and yet so evident and near, we thank you that you are at work in us before we think of asking. We thank you that you hold us by the hand and lead us before we are aware of it. Stay with us in this way and awaken our hearts at the right moment, that we are not surprised by the painful things we experience but can be prepared at all times to watch and pray, trusting that we are not forsaken in the constant strife on this earth. Grant us hope, O God, that the time is coming when all men will hear the proclamation, "See, a new heaven and a new earth, because you have learned to see God's honor in everything." Amen.

21
April

He rescues me unharmed from the battle waged against me, even though many oppose me. PSALM 55:18

Dear Father in heaven, grant that we may come into your presence as your children. Give to us all that we need each day, so that we are no longer caught in the turmoil of life but can receive your peace. For you care for us as your children, and we are allowed to go confidently through all the troubles of these times because our way leads to you, the eternal Father in heaven. Keep us from going astray and from spending our efforts on what is temporal and cannot last. Let your light strengthen us in what is of heaven, in what is eternally true for our lives. Amen.

22

April

Be dressed ready for service and keep your lamps burning, like servants waiting for their master to return from a wedding banquet, so that when he comes and knocks they can immediately open the door for him. LUKE 12:35–36

Lord our God, we wait in expectation. Even in the great distress on earth, we wait in longing for your day to come, for the pangs of death to pass, so that your kingdom may arise and the reign of Jesus Christ may spread over the whole world in power and glory. May your promise be fulfilled and your will be done on earth. May there always be people who believe and who pray in faith, "Lord God, come! Come, Lord God. Humankind does not understand how to live. Send us Jesus Christ, the Savior, Lord, and Judge of the dead and the living. Put an end to sin and death!" We thank you for giving us this faith and for letting us pray at all times, "Come, Lord Jesus. Yes, come soon, Lord Jesus!" We ask you to protect us in this faith. Bring this faith to fulfillment for the glory of your name. Amen.

23

April

I wait for your salvation, O Lord. GENESIS 49:18, NRSV

Lord our God, help us in these days that are so difficult for us. Help us never to lose our expectation of the time that is to come, the time of Jesus Christ, Lord of heaven and earth. Strengthen us, we pray, and strengthen those all over the world who have to endure great suffering, especially the destitute and the dying. May your heavenly hosts come down to the many who are in misery, so that your name is praised in life and in death, in whatever we have to go through. For we shall praise you, no matter what happens now or in the days ahead. May your glory remain in our hearts, with the joy that you, O God, are the Father of all. Amen.

24
April

We also have the prophetic message as something completely reliable, and you will do well to pay attention to it, as to a light shining in a dark place, until the day dawns and the morning star rises in your hearts.

2 PETER 1:19

Lord God, we thank you for giving us light here on earth, where it is so often completely dark. But in the darkness the name of Jesus Christ shines out as the prophetic Word: "Be comforted. After darkness comes light, after night comes day!" We thank you for this light. In joy we thank you, for we have experienced that Jesus lives and comes to meet each one, bringing victory over enemy powers. In the name of Jesus Christ and in his name alone we ask you to remember the needs of our time. We do not want anything that comes from ourselves. We do not want any earthly peace. We want your peace, Lord God, the peace in which everything becomes new, born anew even in suffering, to the eternal glory of your name. Amen.

25
April

When I saw him, I fell at his feet as though dead. Then he placed his right hand on me and said: "Do not be afraid. I am the First and the Last. I am the Living One; I was dead, and now look, I am alive for ever and ever! And I hold the keys of death and Hades."

REVELATION 1:17–18

Lord our God, we thank you with all our hearts that Jesus Christ still lives today and that we may believe in him and call upon him as our Savior. We thank you for him who sees to the depths of our human misery and calls right into the midst of it, "Do not be afraid. I am with you. I live. I am your helper. No matter how insignificant you are, fear not, for I, Jesus Christ, shine into all the darkness, even into the darkness of sin and death, into all the judgment that has fallen or is still to come upon everyone on Earth." Praise to your name, Lord our God! You are great and almighty and beyond our understanding. But you have sent us the Savior whom we can understand, and we rejoice that we may have community with him in your presence. Amen.

26

April

It is good to praise the Lord and make music to your name, O Most High, proclaiming your love in the morning and your faithfulness at night. PSALM 92:1–2

We thank you, Lord our God. How much good you have poured out on us throughout our lives! And how much we should thank you every day! We thank you that again and again we feel your help and know that you can fill our earthly life with what is of heaven. May your kingdom come over the whole world, for all people are longing for faith and for mercy and are to be gathered into your house under the staff of the Good Shepherd, Jesus Christ. Watch over us during the night. May your help go far and wide into the whole world. Stand by those who call upon you, even when they do not understand how they should pray. Help us and grant that the Savior may come, to the glory of your name. Amen.

27 April

On the day I called, you answered me, you increased my strength of soul. PSALM 138:3, NRSV

Dear Father in heaven, we thank you that we are your children and that your eyes watch over us and see all that is in our hearts. You hear the request of each heart, and you will answer at the right time. Stretch out your strong hand to us, for we are weak and often heavy-hearted, not knowing what to do nor how to find you. But you are with us in every need in spite of all our faults and shortcomings. You are with us; you lead us through everything to our life's true goal, until each of us can rejoice over all you have done, to the praise of your name, our Father. Amen.

28

April

You make known to me the path of life; you will fill me with joy in your presence, with eternal pleasures at your right hand. PSALM 16:11

Dear Father in heaven, you show us the way of life; in your presence is fullness of joy, and at your right hand is delight forever. In your presence we want to rejoice together as your children, under your protection. May we become firm in every part of our life on earth. Grant that soon something of your kingdom, of your heaven, may encircle us like a blessing, enabling us to fight on in joy and exultation. We entrust ourselves to you, our faithful and loving God, and we thank you. Amen.

29
April

The Lord is a refuge for the oppressed, a stronghold in times of trouble. Those who know your name trust in you, for you, Lord, have never forsaken those who seek you. PSALM 9:9–10

Lord our God, we look to you in our many needs, in the distress of our hearts, in the anguish of the whole world. We beseech you, let light come to your people everywhere on earth to bring them your help and your victory. Remember the wretched, the sick, the poor. Let your living strength come to them so that they can bear their sufferings and hold out joyfully to the end. Remember us all, O Lord our God, for we all need you. We are weak and poor and cannot go forward alone. Your Spirit must help us. May the Savior come to us, and may his grace and his power be born in our hearts. Amen.

30

April

He withdrew about a stone's throw beyond them, knelt down and prayed, "Father, if you are willing, take this cup from me; yet not my will, but yours be done."

LUKE 22:41–42

Dear Father in heaven, we lift our eyes to you. You allow earthly events to follow their own course, and even your own Son had to suffer and die. But your plan is already prepared and you will act in our time according to your will. We pray, "Your will be done, your will!" In the midst of all the suffering let your love be revealed in many places, wherever it is possible for people to understand it. You have always protected us; protect us still. You have done much for us and we want to praise your name. We want to be people who always acknowledge you and praise you, for you will never let any be lost who hope in you. Be with us this night, help us, and send us the strength we need to serve you, also in our everyday life. Amen.

✦ ✦ ✦

May

1

May

"For I know the plans I have for you," declares the Lord, "plans to prosper you and not to harm you, plans to give you hope and a future." JEREMIAH 29:11

Lord Jesus, we look to you on the throne beside your Father in heaven and ask that you be Lord of peace in our hearts. Help us to overcome ourselves again and again and to remain at peace. Then your will may be done in your disciples, a power of peace may be around us that goes out into the whole world, and your name may be glorified on earth. For you are Lord of peace, and we await you. In difficult times faith and hope will take hold in our hearts all the more firmly, to your glory, Lord Jesus. For you will suddenly come according to your promise as the One who does God's will on earth among all people. Amen.

2

May

I cry to you, Lord; I say, "You are my refuge, my portion in the land of the living." PSALM 142:5

Lord our God, we seek your light and pray that you shed your light upon us so that we live not only on earth but in you, the eternal and living One. May our lives be drawn into eternity, to the praise of your name, O Father. May we take your Word to heart so that we can become true men and women, able to bear everything in your name and to remain in the love you want to give us. Rouse us to become true men and women at the side of Jesus Christ our Savior, who has been patient in all things with all people. Be with us at all times, Lord our God. You are our help and our refuge. Amen.

3

May

But how is it to your credit if you receive a beating for doing wrong and endure it? But if you suffer for doing good and you endure it, this is commendable before God. To this you were called, because Christ suffered for you, leaving you an example, that you should follow in his steps. I PETER 2:20–21

Dear Father in heaven, we thank you that the Savior has been with us on the earth and that in our day we can still follow him and wait for your will and your rulership. For you are Almighty God, and your kingdom must come, your will be done, and all promises be fulfilled. Carry out your will, we beseech you. Establish your kingdom among all nations, even if today this is possible with only a few. For through your working, hearts can change so that your name may be praised and all promises be fulfilled. Thank you for allowing us to live in such great hope. Stay by us in our work on earth so that it may be done in your service. In every situation deepen our longing for the Savior to come and establish your kingdom. Be with us during the night and bless us in your great goodness and faithfulness. Amen.

4

May

The Lord replied, "My Presence will go with you, and I will give you rest." EXODUS 33:14

Dear Father in heaven, we thank you for guiding us on all our ways with power from on high. We thank you that again and again you have led us through the darkness on a path of light. Looking back, we cannot be thankful enough. May our hearts turn to you and be filled with quiet certainty in all we are still awaiting. Remember us and remember the many who lie under heavy bondage. Let the time come when you will bring a great deliverance to those who are in darkness. Then we can find meaning for our lives in all that happens, knowing that you have been faithful in everything. You have done more than we asked, more than we can understand. Amen.

5
May

I am unworthy of all the kindness and faithfulness you have shown your servant. I had only my staff when I crossed this Jordan, but now I have become two camps.

GENESIS 32:10

Lord our God, we are not worthy of all the mercy and faithfulness you show to us. We thank you for your love and ask you to keep our hearts united in the hope we have together for all things. Keep our hearts united, that again and again we can receive something new from your mighty hand. Keep us true to the calling you have given us. Let light shine out into the world, right into the dark places. Remember those all over the world who are sighing to you, longing that in your great and wonderful goodness light may come to the peoples and to the nations through some deed from your hand. Amen.

6

May

And I heard a loud voice from the throne saying, "Look! God's dwelling place is now among the people, and he will dwell with them. They will be his people, and God himself will be with them and be their God. He will wipe every tear from their eyes. There will be no more death or mourning or crying or pain, for the old order of things has passed away." REVELATION 21:3–4

Lord our God, we look to you and to Jesus Christ our Savior. Continually renew your grace and your power in our lives, we pray. Renew your grace and power, that we may have light even in dark and distressing times and through the Savior may overcome as we wait faithfully for your kingdom. Help us to be ready to take anything upon ourselves, to serve you with body and soul, with all we have and are. May we belong to the hosts of those who go to meet you, who wait for your coming kingdom, which will bring comfort to the world and to all people who now suffer and grieve. O Lord our God, have mercy on our times and on our world. Grant that with thanks and praise we may soon see the signs of the fulfillment of your promises. Amen.

7

May

This is how we know that we live in him and he in us: He has given us of his Spirit. 1 JOHN 4:13

Dear Father in heaven, we thank you with all our hearts because we know you are holding us by your hand and leading us on all our ways, in spite of all contradiction, strife, distress, and confusion within ourselves. What are all these compared to your love, which does not let us go but watches over us and finally brings us to what is good? Release us from our many burdens. Free our spirits and our souls more and more until we can do nothing but give praise and thanks with heart, soul, and strength for all you are to us. Amen.

8

May

God is our refuge and strength, an ever-present help in trouble... The Lord Almighty is with us; the God of Jacob is our fortress. PSALM 46:1, 7

Lord, Almighty God of heaven and earth, grant that we may come to you as your children. For you have chosen us through the gospel, and Jesus Christ has obtained mercy for us so that in you we have a refuge in disturbed and evil times. We turn to your Word, Lord God, rejoicing that again and again the whole of Christendom is led back to your Word. Strengthen all those who serve your Word, who look to you and to the grace of Jesus Christ. Grant that everywhere we may have hope and joy in the redemption you will bring in every situation, also in our ordinary practical life. Grant that through this redemption the earth may proclaim your praise and honor your name, your kingdom may come, and your will be done on earth as in heaven. Amen.

9
May

The sun will no more be your light by day, nor will the brightness of the moon shine on you, for the Lord will be your everlasting light, and your God will be your glory.

ISAIAH 60:19

Lord, our God and Father, we thank you that in all the misery and night on earth you have let your hope dawn as a light shining for all your people – all who honor your name, all who dwell in Jesus Christ through forgiveness of sins and through resurrection to a new life. Praise to your name. Praise to Jesus Christ. Praise to the Holy Spirit, who can comfort, teach, and guide our hearts. O Father in heaven, we can never thank you enough that we are allowed to be a people full of grace, full of hope, and full of confidence that your kingdom is coming at last to bring salvation and peace for the whole world. Amen.

10

May

Oh, that salvation for Israel would come out of Zion! When the Lord restores his people, let Jacob rejoice and Israel be glad! PSALM 14:7

Lord our God, our Father in heaven, bless us who have become united in our hope in you and in our expectation of your help on this earth, where people live in all kinds of foolish ways. Bless your Word within us. Grant us your Holy Spirit to restore life and gladness to our hearts, even in grief and suffering. Grant this not only in the distress of the whole world, but also in our own lives as long as we remain on this earth. Let signs be seen on every hand that you help us and give us a strength we can rely on. You help us in all circumstances every day, every year, ever anew. For this we thank you and praise your name. Amen.

11
May

For you died, and your life is now hidden with Christ in God. When Christ, who is your life, appears, then you also will appear with him in glory. COLOSSIANS 3:3–4

Lord our God, we thank you for making us into a community whose refuge and certainty is Jesus Christ. We thank you that he will not remain hidden from us forever; his life will be revealed, perhaps soon, in our times. Lord God, how long, how long have your children waited! Now a new time is coming, the end of this age, and we rejoice in this even if you must also judge and punish. No matter what happens, we are at peace. We live in your future, in the future of Jesus Christ, in the great day when humankind will receive the Spirit and their old works will come to an end. Be with us. Bless us this night and help us in what we have most on our hearts. We have so much on our hearts, but you see everything and you know our needs. Lord God, your grace will overcome all earthly troubles, and your name will be glorified on earth if only there is a church that believes and truly awaits your help. Praise to your name! Amen.

12

May

Jesus replied, "Anyone who loves me will obey my teaching. My Father will love them, and we will come to them and make our home with them." JOHN 14:23

Lord our God, we thank you that we can be children of your Spirit. We thank you that because you have called us, we receive eternal gifts that enable us to stand firm even when many sorrows and burdens weigh us down. For you are our life, and in all the darkness, even that of death, you give us light and strength and joyful hope. Keep these alive in us. May an ever brighter light shine on all that you have already put into our hearts, on all that draws us daily to you. Amen.

13

May

For God, who said, "Let light shine out of darkness," made his light shine in our hearts to give us the light of the knowledge of God's glory displayed in the face of Christ. 2 CORINTHIANS 4:6

Lord our God, whose light shines out of the darkness and gleams brightly into our hearts, we thank you for all the goodness you allow us to see. We want to see your goodness clearly and have confidence in it, no matter how much around us is dark and disquieting. We want to remain firm and full of trust, looking to what you have put into our hearts so that we may come to know you. Be with us with your Spirit. Lead us to realize ever more clearly that we are made for your honor. Amen.

14

May

Therefore, since we have been justified through faith, we have peace with God through our Lord Jesus Christ, through whom we have gained access by faith into this grace in which we now stand. And we boast in the hope of the glory of God. ROMANS 5:1–2

Lord our God, almighty and holy One, whose glory shines upon the earth so that we may find joy in you and may live rejoicing in all your loving-kindness, spread out your hands in blessing over all people. Spread your blessing over the happy and the sad, over the courageous and the weak. Shepherd them in your love, in the great grace you have given through Jesus Christ, confirmed in us through the Holy Spirit. Do not let us remain degraded and worthless. Lift our hearts above what is transitory, for you have given us something eternal to live by. Help us every day so that we can reach the goal you have set for us, for many others, and finally for all peoples of the earth. Amen.

15
May

Know that the Lord is God. It is he who made us, and we are his; we are his people, the sheep of his pasture.

PSALM 100:3

Father in heaven, may we recognize and acknowledge that you are God. You have made us, and not we ourselves, to be your people and the sheep of your pasture. Baptize us with the truth we need throughout our lives. Give us the gift to discern who we are and what we should become. Free our eyes from all deception so that we can no longer delude ourselves with short-lived, earthly things. Clear our eyes to see what is eternal in and around us. Make us children, true children, who awake to exult and rejoice in what is childlike and who give thanks to you, O God, the Father, the Son, and the Holy Spirit. Amen.

16

May

Now this is eternal life: that they know you, the only true God, and Jesus Christ, whom you have sent. JOHN 17:3

Lord God, we thank you that you have revealed life in Jesus Christ. Grant that we may enter this life through the grace you have given us to recognize Jesus Christ as our Lord, to believe in him, and to hope for all the good still to come as the fruit of his suffering and resurrection. May the glory of the Living One be revealed to the dead throughout the whole world so that even the dead and the unbelieving may be awakened and see his life. Keep us true to what you have given us. Strengthen our faith and endurance in all our trials. Let your name soon be honored among all people so that hatred may cease and the coming of your great day may be foretold in changed hearts and changed thoughts. Protect us this night. Bless us and help us again and again as you have promised. Amen.

17
May

Therefore, since we have a great high priest who has ascended into heaven, Jesus the Son of God, let us hold firmly to the faith we profess. For we do not have a high priest who is unable to empathize with our weaknesses, but we have one who has been tempted in every way, just as we are – yet he did not sin. HEBREWS 4:14–15

Dear Father in heaven, we look to Jesus Christ, who is at your right hand, through whom you have promised help for the whole world. Unite us with him so that we may receive authority to help all people according to your will. May your name be kept holy among us, for your children have every reason to rejoice in the Savior you have given them. We thank you for everything you have shown to those who believe in you. We pray to you, hasten the time when your day shall come with glory, the day when you will give the glory to Jesus Christ, when he will reign and triumph over all evil and bring the peace you have always wanted to give the world. We wait and long for this. Amen.

18

May

And by him we cry, "Abba, Father." The Spirit himself testifies with our spirit that we are God's children. Now if we are children, then we are heirs – heirs of God and co-heirs with Christ, if indeed we share in his sufferings in order that we may also share in his glory.

ROMANS 8:15B–17

Lord our God, Father of us all, grant that we may know something of you in our hearts. Each one of us is different, with his own particular needs, but we are all your children and should all become children of your Spirit. Then even in the difficulties of life, in the many struggles, temptations, and sorrows, we can keep up our courage and remain in the Spirit, who is victorious in every aspect of life. Protect and strengthen us on all our ways. We praise you for all you have done and for all the help you have given us. Amen.

19

May

I love you, Lord, my strength. The Lord is my rock, my fortress and my deliverer; my God is my rock, in whom I take refuge, my shield and the horn of my salvation, my stronghold. PSALM 18:1–2

Lord our God, we thank you that we have often felt you close to us. We thank you that you are near us and that you strengthen the weak. Remember us and give each one the help he needs to be true to his calling. Remember all humankind and grant that we may go forward in spirit and in truth. Give new light to the peoples who are still in great darkness. Let your kingdom and your reign be revealed and your name at last be honored by all. Amen.

20
May

This is good, and pleases God our Savior, who wants all people to be saved and to come to a knowledge of the truth. 1 TIMOTHY 2:3–4

Lord our God, give us your Spirit, we pray, that we may learn to understand what we are and what tasks you have set for us. We thank you for all the light you give us. Grant that we and many others may come closer to knowledge of the truth and be at peace about all that belongs in your hands, our Father in heaven. Keep us now and forevermore in your almighty hand. May we know your goodness and the blessing it brings. For through your goodness we can endure even the hardest days and be victorious in the battle of life. Amen.

21

May

For I am not ashamed of the gospel, because it is the power of God that brings salvation to everyone who believes: first to the Jew, then to the Gentile. For in the gospel the righteousness of God is revealed – a righteousness that is by faith from first to last, just as it is written: "The righteous will live by faith." ROMANS 1:16–17

Lord our God, you have revealed your righteousness to us in the gospel, your righteousness that comes to us through faith and continues in faith. Grant that we may understand your righteousness and live by it even in a crooked generation. Then to our joy the gospel will bear fruit. Protect us in the midst of temptation and conflicting opinions so that we are raised above them and remain free, with our thoughts on you and your true and loving righteousness. Your righteousness gives us hope for the many, many people who still need help to realize that their lives are not of passing value but of eternal worth. Amen.

22

May

I will declare your name to my people; in the assembly I will praise you. PSALM 22:22

Lord our God, Almighty Father in heaven, we stand before you as your children, whom you want to protect through the need of our time, through all sin and death. We praise you for giving us so much peace in an age full of trouble, and for granting us the assurance of your help. Even when we suffer, we do not want to remain in the darkness of suffering but want to rise up to praise and glorify you. For your kingdom is coming; it is already at hand. Your kingdom comforts and helps us and points the way for the whole world, that your will may be done on earth as in heaven. Amen.

23
May

They are not of the world, even as I am not of it. Sanctify them by the truth; your word is truth. JOHN 17:16–17

Dear God and Father of us all, sanctify us in your truth. Your Word is truth. We come before your presence and ask you to touch us with your Spirit, to shape our lives in the truth and in the joy of your name. Touch us with your Spirit, that we may carry out our tasks in your service. May your face shine on us and on all needy people who turn to you. May your power be given ever more fully, and may your cause become great in the world until at last it brings new life to all nations. Amen.

24

May

The Spirit of the Lord is on me, because he has anointed me to proclaim good news to the poor. He has sent me to proclaim freedom for the prisoners and recovery of sight for the blind, to set the oppressed free, to proclaim the year of the Lord's favor. LUKE 4:18–19

We thank you, dear Father in heaven, for the many times you let us experience that we do not need to despair because of darkness, weakness, or sickness. You hear the desires of our hearts. You love us for all that we love when we love the Savior and when we praise his name. Let us remain in this spirit. Come to us with many proofs of your power, to the glory of your name. Come in the inner quiet of heart through which we are able to grasp what it means for us that you are our Father in Jesus Christ. Amen.

25

May

God is faithful, who has called you into fellowship with his Son, Jesus Christ our Lord. I CORINTHIANS 1:9

Lord our God, we stand before you and rejoice that we may have fellowship with you through the Lord Jesus Christ. Grant us the light of your Spirit. Grant our hearts strength for life. Open for us the paths of life, that we may find joy and hope in spite of all the suffering we must go through on earth. Let all humankind be entrusted to your care. Rule over them with your power, whether they are aware of it or not, and take world history into your hands so that all people may receive your mercy. Amen.

26

May

Blessed are the poor in spirit, for theirs is the kingdom of heaven. MATTHEW 5:3

Dear Father in heaven, we thank you for wanting to give us happiness and for holding our earthly life firmly in your hands. May we have the confidence that we are in your hands. Grant us the light of faith. Let this light of faith guide us in material things and help us to wait in patience until the doors open for us to pass through according to your pleasure. So bless us all. Bless our life. May we grow joyful and free of heart through all that Jesus Christ gives. On the foundation he establishes for us may your divine working, your fatherly love, lift and support us throughout our lives. Amen.

27

May

May the grace of the Lord Jesus Christ, and the love of God, and the fellowship of the Holy Spirit be with you all. 2 CORINTHIANS 13:14

Lord our God, our Father in heaven, we thank you for letting us receive so much that is good in all circumstances on earth. We thank you that we can have joy in life in spite of our shortcomings, mistakes, and worries. You bless us with heavenly gifts, so that rejoicing, we can walk on earth as if in heaven. Keep the gifts of your Spirit alive in us. Keep alive in us everything that Jesus Christ was, everything he is, and everything he will be on earth for all people. Amen.

28
May

You are all children of the light and children of the day. We do not belong to the night or to the darkness. So then, let us not be like others, who are asleep, but let us be awake and sober. I THESSALONIANS 5:5–6

Dear Father in heaven, we thank you that we may be your children. We thank you that through your Spirit our hearts may know that we are your children. Even when everything around us becomes difficult and we are hemmed in by darkness, we remain your children. Even when we often do not see how we are to go on and everything seems to be taken from us, we remain your children. Even when sin and death surround us and accuse us of being in the wrong, we still remain your children. As your children we entrust ourselves to your hands. In our whole life, in all our work and activity, we dwell in what has come from you, and we rejoice in Christ our Savior. Amen.

29
May

But because of his great love for us, God, who is rich in mercy, made us alive with Christ even when we were dead in transgressions – it is by grace you have been saved. And God raised us up with Christ and seated us with him in the heavenly realms in Christ Jesus.

EPHESIANS 2:4–6

Lord our God, we thank you for allowing us to experience your power. We thank you that we need not be occupied with material things only. We thank you that your Spirit comes to our aid again and again. Grant that we may continue to have your help, and let many hearts find what a grace it is that in spirit we may walk in heaven even during this transitory life with all its foolish ways. We may say with complete assurance that everything tormenting and burdening will pass by. It passes by, and we go joyfully and confidently toward your kingdom, which continually gains in power. Amen.

30

May

Praise the Lord, my soul; all my inmost being, praise his holy name. Praise the Lord, my soul, and forget not all his benefits – who forgives all your sins and heals all your diseases. PSALM 103:1–3

Lord our God, O Holy One, we thank you that we may lay aside our own nature and be lifted in spirit above all that is temporal and human and have joy in you. In spite of all the evil surrounding us, in spite of the thousandfold misery of humankind, we may still rejoice in you, in all you do and will yet do for us. Grant that we may go on rejoicing, having joy together, helping instead of burdening each other, until this earth is filled with the jubilation of those you have so richly blest. Forgive us all our sins. Heal us in mind and body. Deliver us from all the corruption that tries to take hold of our souls. Amen.

31
May

As for you, see that what you have heard from the beginning remains in you. If it does, you also will remain in the Son and in the Father. And this is what he promised us – eternal life. I JOHN 2:24–25

Lord our God, we want to find our joy in you and in all your promises to us. For you have promised that in the midst of all the pain and sorrow, you are preparing what pleases you and serves your honor in every heart. May we experience in our lives the fulfillment of many of your promises, so that again and again we can go forward joyfully, rising above difficult times and situations. Have mercy on us and protect us in your strength. Amen.

June

1

June

For the bread of God is the bread that comes down from heaven and gives life to the world. JOHN 6:33

Dear Father in heaven, in your Word we trust, in your Word of eternal life, given us in Jesus Christ our Savior. We build on this Word of life in these days when it seems that everything is losing strength and value, and yet there is so much longing in people's hearts. You will not let our hope be disappointed. What you have spoken must be fulfilled. What is promised in Jesus Christ must come into being, not only for a few but for the whole world, for which he died and was raised from the dead. Be with us. Keep us so fully alive that our lives reflect all the goodness we are allowed to experience and we overcome all the evil which tries to attack us. We thank you for calling us to life and for renewing us again and again. May your name be praised among us forever. Amen.

2

June

Praise the Lord, my soul. Lord my God, you are very great; you are clothed with splendor and majesty. The Lord wraps himself in light as with a garment; he stretches out the heavens like a tent. PSALM 104:1–2

Lord our God, our Father in heaven, with all our hearts we want to thank you for giving us joy on earth and for sending us your radiant light from heaven. We praise you for the light you give our hearts, the light that lets us find great joy together because we become one in you, one in your Spirit, one in awaiting your promised good. Grant that we may be your children. May we always find the paths where you can go with us and give us what we cannot give ourselves. May our whole life glorify you and our every breath belong to you. Through communion with you may we remain in your safekeeping in body, soul, and spirit. For all you have done and for all you will do for us, we ask you to accept our thanks. Amen.

3

June

He came and preached peace to you who were far away and peace to those who were near. For through him we both have access to the Father by one Spirit.

EPHESIANS 2:17–18

Dear Father in heaven, we thank you for all your goodness and for the peace you give us. Unite us as your people, we pray. Unite us as one people with all your children who have ever lived, as one people with all who want to serve you. The more faithfully and joyfully we are your people, the more blessing you can give. Let the material world come under your hand. Guide your children on earth. Lead us in such a way that others may be helped. When we suffer, grant us strength and understanding of your will. Protect us today and every day. Amen.

4

June

Because of the Lord's great love we are not consumed, for his compassions never fail. They are new every morning; great is your faithfulness. I say to myself, "The Lord is my portion; therefore I will wait for him."

LAMENTATIONS 3:22–24

Dear Father in heaven, we thank you for guiding us, your children, here on earth. We thank you that whatever happens to us, we can again and again find joy because you give us what is good even when times are evil and when we go through sorrow. We thank you that your goodness and your faithfulness penetrate everything, and that at last, at long last, they penetrate our hearts. Then we can know and be glad that your Spirit guides us. We can know we are never alone but can receive strength to help us in the struggle and toil of our life. Through your help everything becomes fruitful – good and evil, life and death, health and suffering. Everything must serve you through the working of your Spirit. Amen.

5
June

Surely God is my salvation; I will trust and not be afraid. The Lord, the Lord himself, is my strength and my defense; he has become my salvation. ISAIAH 12:2

Dear Father in heaven, we thank you that you are so near us and that we may be near you. We thank you that throughout our days we may be people who listen to you with all our hearts and minds, a listening people who can receive what is good and true for our lives and who can witness to the power you give us through the Savior. Protect us in all things. Look into our hearts and into the situation of each one of us, where many things are still faulty and unclear. Deliver us from evil, for the kingdom shall be yours. From you the power shall come. Your glory shall radiate from our lives, and we shall praise and thank you forevermore. Amen.

6

June

I will sing of the Lord's great love forever; with my mouth I will make your faithfulness known through all generations. I will declare that your love stands firm forever, that you have established your faithfulness in heaven itself. PSALM 89:1–2

Lord our God, gather us together in one flock to praise you with one heart and one voice. Let this praise ring out on earth in the midst of all the evils that still confront us. We thank you for your protection, for all the help and deliverance you give us. We thank you for the hope you put into our hearts. We thank you for the hope that we may yet see great things done through the working of your Spirit, for us your children and for all peoples and nations. For your love will not rest until life on earth has come into your hands and all may rejoice. Amen.

7

June

Lord, you have been our dwelling place throughout all generations. Before the mountains were born or you brought forth the whole world, from everlasting to everlasting you are God. PSALM 90:1–2

Lord our God, our refuge forever, bless us who have gathered in your presence and who turn to you in all distress, not only in our personal need but also in the distress of the nations and peoples of the whole world. Grant that we may be your children, with a simple faith that gives us strength to go on working even when life is bitterly hard. We thank you for giving us so much grace, for helping us and never forsaking us, so that again and again we can find joy and can glorify and praise you, our Father. May your name be praised from heaven above and among us here below. May your name be praised by all people throughout the world, and may everyone on earth acknowledge you and receive all that they need from you. Amen.

8
June

The prospect of the righteous is joy, but the hopes of the wicked come to nothing. PROVERBS 10:28

Lord our God, we wait for you night and day. We believe in you and we long for your righteousness. You will answer our prayer. Bless us, we pray. May your name be kept holy and your kingdom come. O Lord our God, may your will be done among the nations. May your will be done in each of us and be plainly seen, as it is in heaven. Look upon the nations. Watch over all humankind. Let a new path be broken so that a peace that passes all understanding may come, a peace from you, the Lord our God. Amen.

9

June

The Lord your God is with you, the Mighty Warrior who saves. He will take great delight in you; in his love he will no longer rebuke you, but will rejoice over you with singing. ZEPHANIAH 3:17

Lord our Savior, you are our Lord and our Helper. Show yourself again and again in our hearts as the Savior who is strong to help us even in difficult times. Remember the many people who sigh to you. Guide them into the protection of the almighty God. Even if they suffer pain and distress and have to go through fear and anxiety, even if they die, Lord Jesus, you are comfort and help. In everything life brings us you will show yourself as the One who does the will of God and who carries it out for us on earth. Amen.

10

June

May God be gracious to us and bless us and make his face shine on us – so that your ways may be known on earth, your salvation among all nations. PSALM 67:1–2

Lord, Almighty God, you are our Father and we are your children, who want to live for you through Jesus Christ our Lord. Strengthen and renew our hearts. When discouragement and fear try to mislead us, may your Holy Spirit help us again and again to hold fast, for no matter what difficulties arise, your will is being done and your will is good. Your name will be honored. Your kingdom will come for all nations. Your reign will come over all peoples, for they are all yours and must acknowledge that Jesus Christ is the Lord, to your honor, O Father. Amen.

11

June

Your love, Lord, reaches to the heavens, your faithfulness to the skies...How priceless is your unfailing love, O God! People take refuge in the shadow of your wings.

PSALM 36:5, 7

Lord our God, we turn our hearts and minds to you. Be with us and grant us your Spirit. May your Word be a blessing for us. We thank you that this Word is given us in Jesus Christ, our Savior. Almighty God, stretch out your hand over the whole world. Let your Spirit bring a new age, an age of truth, righteousness, and love, an age of peace that comes from you. O Lord God, we are your children, and as your children we pray to you in the name of Jesus Christ. You will hear us, and we look forward with joy to the time when all promises will be fulfilled, the time spoken about by the prophets, and especially by your Son, Jesus Christ. Be with us and gather us in your Spirit. Amen.

12
June

When he comes, he will prove the world to be in the wrong about sin and righteousness and judgment: about sin, because people do not believe in me; about righteousness, because I am going to the Father, where you can see me no longer; and about judgment, because the prince of this world now stands condemned. JOHN 16:8–11

Lord our God, we thank you that you continually renew your Spirit in us. We thank you that your Spirit enables us to understand Jesus Christ and to follow him all our days on earth. Bless us, and let your Spirit come to the world, to all people, a new outpouring of the Holy Spirit in each heart. But there must still be punishment for sin. For the sake of justice the world has to suffer punishment through judgment. For you, Almighty God, are Lord, and not even Satan, the prince of this world, can act against your will. You will carry out your will through the Holy Spirit. Our task is simply to follow Jesus all our days. This shall be our joy. Praise to your name that every day, even through great distress, we can joyfully follow him in the strength of the Holy Spirit. Amen.

13

June

I do not hide your righteousness in my heart; I speak of your faithfulness and your saving help. I do not conceal your love and your faithfulness from the great assembly.

PSALM 40:10

Lord our God, in the grace of Jesus Christ we turn to you, our Father in heaven and on earth, for we know your truth and your saving power. Grant that all may learn to look upward to you in faith and in trust that your will is being done on earth, even though so much seems to be the work of humans alone. But your will is behind everything and we put ourselves under your will. We hope in your will. In your will we are certain that everything will be made right and good, to the glory of your name. Amen.

14

June

In fact, this is love for God: to keep his commands. And his commands are not burdensome, for everyone born of God overcomes the world. This is the victory that has overcome the world, even our faith. Who is it that overcomes the world? Only the one who believes that Jesus is the Son of God. 1 JOHN 5:3–5

Lord our God, in the grace of Jesus Christ we pray to you that your will may be done for us and for all the world. Through Jesus Christ grant us faith that you love us, faith that we may live in your love, that we may hope in your love every day and have peace on earth, where there is so much unrest and trouble. Keep us firm and constant, remaining in your peace and in the inner quiet you give us because Jesus Christ has overcome the world. He has truly overcome, and this fills us with joy. We praise you, Almighty God, that you have sent Jesus Christ and that he has overcome the world. We praise you that he has overcome all evil, sin, and death, and that we may rejoice at all times in your presence. Amen.

15

June

The Word became flesh and made his dwelling among us. We have seen his glory, the glory of the one and only Son, who came from the Father, full of grace and truth... Out of his fullness we have all received grace in place of grace already given. JOHN 1:14, 16

Lord God, help us come with all our hearts to the Savior, who leads us into your arms. Hear our pleading and let your countenance shine over the world. Send a new age soon, a new salvation to the earth. Show us that what we have learned about you is the truth, that we may live in the truth and find the way through to heaven. Hear us, O God. Often it seems that you are far away. But we know that our voices still reach you and that those roused by your Holy Spirit will become workers for the Lord Jesus. Send your Spirit soon, O Lord God. Send the Comforter, who leads us into all light and all truth. We entrust ourselves and our daily lives to you. We want to be faithful. Help us to remember at every step that we belong to you, Lord God. No matter how dark it is on earth, help us remember that we are your children. Amen.

16

June

My Father's house has many rooms; if that were not so, would I have told you that I am going there to prepare a place for you? And if I go and prepare a place for you, I will come back and take you to be with me that you also may be where I am. JOHN 14:2–3

Lord God, we thank you that you have upheld us and brought us to the Savior. Help us to remember this truth through your Holy Spirit, and constantly remind us while still on earth to live in heaven with all your angels. We are helpless without you. Your Spirit alone can overcome our sinful nature so that we never forget to be in heaven with the Savior now and in eternity. Amen.

17

June

"The time has come," he said. "The kingdom of God has come near. Repent and believe the good news!" MARK 1:15

Lord our God, we come into your presence and bow down before you, the Almighty. We come before you and repent, believing in you and in your will to save us. Your will to save goes out over the whole world, over the whole godless world, that all may repent and be redeemed. Grant us the thoughts of your heart so that we may begin to understand your will. We dedicate ourselves to you, the holy, just, righteous, and merciful God. Grant that we may be your children, led and guided by you every day. Turn our hearts to you so that you can make us more and more as you want us to be. Turn our hearts to you until your goal of atonement and redemption is reached through the quiet working of your almighty power. Amen.

18
June

So do not be ashamed of the testimony about our Lord or of me his prisoner. Rather, join with me in suffering for the gospel, by the power of God. He has saved us and called us to a holy life – not because of anything we have done but because of his own purpose and grace. This grace was given us in Christ Jesus before the beginning of time. 2 TIMOTHY 1:8–9

Lord our God, radiant, light giving, and almighty God through all the ages, be with us in our time too. Strengthen the grace we have received from Jesus Christ, and let it be known over all the world so that your name may be honored everywhere. Bless us, we pray, and let your blessing spread from us to others, to the glory of your name. Grant that the good may be strengthened in us, the good you have let us hear about for so many years. May everything that belongs to your Word come alive in us and in the world. May your blessing be on our actions, for we want to remain under your blessing, to the glory of your righteousness and truth. Amen.

19

June

"Though the mountains be shaken and the hills be removed, yet my unfailing love for you will not be shaken nor my covenant of peace be removed," says the Lord, who has compassion on you. ISAIAH 54:10

Lord, O great and almighty God, we thank you that you have given us the Savior, in whom we can become united and have peace on earth. May he, the Savior, work powerfully among us. May your Spirit come into people's hearts so that they learn to acknowledge you as their leader and their God and to rejoice in their lives, which are intended for eternal life. Bless us through your Word and through all the good you do for us. Constantly renew and strengthen us in faith and in patience through the grace you send us. Remember all the peoples who should become yours in the name of Jesus Christ. May they all confess that Jesus Christ is the Lord, to the honor of God the Father. We praise you for the promise you have given us of a wonderful new day of help for all. We praise you that you have created all people to recognize their true calling and their way to salvation. Amen.

20

June

But since we belong to the day, let us be sober, putting on faith and love as a breastplate, and the hope of salvation as a helmet. For God did not appoint us to suffer wrath but to receive salvation through our Lord Jesus Christ.

I THESSALONIANS 5:8–9

Lord God Almighty, bring in the day, the day of Jesus Christ, through whom we shall be united. Then we shall recognize each other as fellow citizens, as brothers and sisters, and we shall have peace on earth. Give your Spirit anew, O Lord our God. Free and enlighten every heart so that each person can acknowledge the Word you have given them and hold fast to all your promises, even in dark and troubled times. Be with us. Be with our people. Help us in our times, O Lord God. We wait for you. We await your peace, a new peace – not the old peace, not a return to comfort and selfish desires, but your peace – which shall bring us into the life of heaven, where we find Jesus Christ, the Living One, our Shepherd and Leader. Amen.

21

June

Father, I want those you have given me to be with me where I am, and to see my glory, the glory you have given me because you loved me before the creation of the world.

JOHN 17:24

Lord our God, we thank you that you have revealed your glory in your Son Jesus Christ. We thank you that today we can still see and feel the glorious grace which streams out from Jesus Christ in his victory over the world, the powerful help which benefits all those who find faith. Grant that a further glory may be revealed, faith dwelling in the hearts of all people, faith that can conquer all the need and suffering on earth, faith that is the power to look to you, to become inwardly quiet in you, and to hope in you at all times. Then your help will come quickly, more quickly than we can imagine. It will come on us unawares, for the Savior has said, "See, I shall come quickly." We want to hope and believe and trust till the end. Amen.

22

June

Again Jesus said, "Peace be with you! As the Father has sent me, I am sending you." JOHN 20:21

Lord our God, in the name of Jesus Christ, who is close at our side as the risen and living One, we lift our eyes to you in prayer. Bless us. Bless us through your Word, and let our hearts become quiet in you. Free us from all restlessness and from the turmoil of the present age, for we belong to you, not to the world. We want to find peace in you and remain in you. You will care for us as your children, whom you will never forget in all eternity. Bless us and renew the riches of your grace in us every day, for you, O Lord our God, remain our Father. Amen.

23
June

Let the peace of Christ rule in your hearts, since as members of one body you were called to peace. And be thankful. COLOSSIANS 3:15

Lord our God, grant your peace in our hearts. Grant that we may be your children, allowed to serve you in true peace through the forgiveness of sins. Turn your eyes to the world and its sin, that something new may come for all who are deeply unhappy, groaning under the anguish of their lives. Your mercy is great, your compassion is beyond measure. For Jesus Christ's sake you will bring into the world the salvation you promised. You will bring the great day of Jesus Christ the Savior, who has shed his blood for us. May he come to those in need and misery, bringing his peace and power into their hearts so that even death turns into life and everything serves your praise and glory. May life from heaven grow in those who understand you and who are to be your people. May your will be done, Lord God, until your kingdom comes in its fullness and all the world may see that Jesus Christ is the Lord, to your glory, O God our Father. Amen.

24
June

I lift up my eyes to you, to you who sit enthroned in heaven. As the eyes of slaves look to the hand of their master, as the eyes of a female slave look to the hand of her mistress, so our eyes look to the Lord our God, till he shows us his mercy. PSALM 123:1–2

Lord our God, we lift our hearts to you, our help in every need. You do so much for us even in difficult times, letting us always see your light and giving us your help in the many things you want us to bear in your strength, O Almighty God. In the end you will help our age come to your light. Through your great mercy let us receive your Word. Bless it within our hearts, and help us to serve you everywhere we go and in everything we are allowed to do. Amen.

25

June

May the God of hope fill you with all joy and peace as you trust in him, so that you may overflow with hope by the power of the Holy Spirit. ROMANS 15:13

Lord our God, grant us courageous hearts, we pray. Grant that we may always find our strength and support in you and may bear with joy whatever the present days bring us. No matter how much evil occurs, we know that your peace is already prepared. We await your peace, and we are allowed to believe that everything will turn out according to your will and according to the good you have prepared for your people on earth. For in faith your people overcome the world, and at last through their faith others too may receive something from you and may lift their eyes to you, the God of truth, of justice, of salvation, and of peace. Be with us every day, Lord God. Help us. Bless us, and bless all who try to bring help where it is needed. Let us praise your name forevermore! Amen.

26

June

We proclaim to you what we have seen and heard, so that you also may have fellowship with us. And our fellowship is with the Father and with his Son, Jesus Christ.

I JOHN 1:3

O Lord our God, grant that we may have fellowship with you every day. May our hearts be ready to fulfill your commandments and to do what you want in all things. Hear our prayer. Hear and answer when we pray for the nations, for the whole world, and let your holy will be done. Remember all who are in distress, and lead them on the right way. May we go with joyful hearts wherever you lead us. Your name will be our help, your glory will come, and the world will be full of your love, your power, and your splendor. Amen.

27

June

But just as he who called you is holy, so be holy in all you do; for it is written: "Be holy, because I am holy."

1 PETER 1:15–16

Lord God, help us to be holy as you are holy, and free us from all the earthly things that try to torment us. Grant us your Spirit so that we do what is right. May we always hold your hand confidently. Protect your children everywhere on earth, and help them do what is right even if the whole world does what is wrong. Help us, so that all we do becomes holy and pleasing in your sight. Let your grace grow among us and among the nations, and let your hand be strong to bring in your day, your day when everything is made new. May your name be kept holy, your kingdom come, and your will be done on earth as in heaven. Amen.

28
June

For the creation waits in eager expectation for the children of God to be revealed. For the creation was subjected to frustration, not by its own choice, but by the will of the one who subjected it, in hope that the creation itself will be liberated from its bondage to decay and brought into the freedom and glory of the children of God.

ROMANS 8:19–21

Lord God, we thank you for all you reveal in your creation so that our lives may be fruitful. Reveal your wisdom and strength among people everywhere so that death and destruction do not have their way, but your will, your love, your mercy shall prevail. Let our age learn that power belongs to you and not to men, and that you will at last fulfill all your promises of good. Your day of justice and holiness will break in, and all misery will be removed through your great mercy. Watch over us as you have done till this hour, and keep us safe during the night. Be present and carry out your will wherever there is misfortune. May your will be done on earth as in heaven. Amen.

29
June

But I will sing of your strength, in the morning I will sing of your love; for you are my fortress, my refuge in times of trouble. You are my strength, I sing praise to you; you, God, are my fortress, my God on whom I can rely. PSALM 59:16–17

Lord God, we glorify your name. How we wish our voices could ring out over all the world, telling of the great things you have done for us, praising you that we can come to you in Jesus Christ, that we can worship, honor, and thank you for all your goodness! Safeguard all your children so that they hold to faith and remain true to the message of the gospel. May we thank and praise you for all you have done this day and for your working in the hearts of many people who are still unknown to us. Your Spirit rules and calls people, to bring them to you, the Father in heaven. Watch over us and continue to bless us. Help us who belong to your people, and protect us through the night. Amen.

30

June

At that time Jesus said, "I praise you, Father, Lord of heaven and earth, because you have hidden these things from the wise and learned, and revealed them to little children." MATTHEW 11:25

Lord our God, we thank you for your Word, which is light and strength to us. We thank you for all you give us. We thank you that we may be counted among the simple-hearted, among the children. We do not want to be anything great in the world. We want only to be with you as your children, helpless little children, watched over by you, the Creator and Father of all. Grant us your blessing. Help us in all that is good and right, also in our daily work, so that we can be your children and do what you have commanded. May your name be honored at all times, your kingdom come, and your will be done on earth as in heaven. Give us today our daily bread. Forgive us the wrong we have done as we forgive those who have wronged us, and lead us not into temptation, but deliver us from evil. For yours is the kingdom, the power, and the glory for ever and ever. Amen.

July

1
July

People will come from east and west and north and south, and will take their places at the feast in the kingdom of God. Indeed there are those who are last who will be first, and first who will be last. LUKE 13:29–30

Dear Father in heaven, Almighty God, grant that the nations come under your rule, under your judgment from morning to evening, from east to west, from north to south. For your will must be done, and your name must be honored among all nations. Yours alone is the kingdom; all kingdoms belong to you. Your heavenly kingdom must come so that at last we learn to be at peace and become your children, who submit to you. For your Christ shall carry out your loving, merciful, and perfect will throughout the world. We thank you for all the good you want to provide for us. May your angels watch over us this night. Be with us in all we do or leave undone. Help us with your strong hands, that we may rejoice at heart in all the good you give us. Amen.

2

July

I instruct you in the way of wisdom and lead you along straight paths. When you walk, your steps will not be hampered; when you run, you will not stumble.

PROVERBS 4:11–12

Dear Father in heaven, you are our God. You rule and guide us, and our trust remains in you even when many needs pull at our hearts and try to draw us into their whirlpool. Protect us, we pray. May your divine hand govern us so that we remain aware of the calling we receive from you and always have a light shining into our lives to show us how to serve you. Let your power work wherever hearts respond to you on this earth, wherever the strength of Jesus Christ is revealed, so that people acknowledge his deeds to your honor. Be with the lowliest and least noticed of your children. Keep them in your hands and enable them to be fellow workers who persevere courageously and confidently until the time when you reveal yourself to all peoples on earth. Amen.

3

July

I am confident of this, that the one who began a good work among you will bring it to completion by the day of Jesus Christ. PHILIPPIANS 1:6, NRSV

Dear Father in heaven, we thank you for the work you are doing. We thank you for working through people of all kinds and of all vocations and through the many hearts that know your goodness. We thank you for the great work led by the Lord Jesus, who will overcome the world with patience and with gentleness. He will overcome the world, opening the door wide for all, including the poorest of the poor, to come to you, their Father in heaven. Grant that with the light we have been given we may remain firm and true. Do not let us come into temptation, but deliver us from evil. For the kingdom, the power, and the glory are yours forever. Amen.

4

July

What, then, shall we say in response to these things? If God is for us, who can be against us? He who did not spare his own Son, but gave him up for us all – how will he not also, along with him, graciously give us all things?

ROMANS 8:31–32

Lord our God, our Father in heaven and on earth, we ask you to bless us, your children, for we want to be your children and nothing else. We want to have our joy and delight in knowing that we belong to you, the almighty God, who began and who will complete redemption on earth through Jesus Christ, our Savior. Bless your Word in us. Give us courage in suffering and distress, for we are allowed to serve you in all circumstances, even when we find it bitterly hard. Your name shall be honored in us, your kingdom shall come. As surely as the earth endures, everything shall happen in accordance with your will, on earth as in heaven. Amen.

5
July

We know that the whole creation has been groaning as in the pains of childbirth right up to the present time. Not only so, but we ourselves, who have the firstfruits of the Spirit, groan inwardly as we wait eagerly for our adoption to sonship, the redemption of our bodies. For in this hope we were saved. ROMANS 8:22–24A

Lord our God, we thank you for the great calling you have given us. We thank you that in all the evils of today's world you give us the hope and faith that you are leading us to a goal that is good, and you make us free. You make your children free so that throughout humankind a new spirit may come, a new life and a new power to serve you in time and eternity. Praise to your name that we can always have hope; nothing can discourage us, but everything must work together for good in accordance with your great purpose. Grant that your compassion may come to all the world, to all peoples, whom you have looked upon with mercy in sending Jesus Christ as Savior. Amen.

6

July

For those who are led by the Spirit of God are the children of God. The Spirit you received does not make you slaves, so that you live in fear again; rather, the Spirit you received brought about your adoption to sonship.

ROMANS 8:14–15A

Dear Father in heaven, open our hearts to the wonder of being able to call you Father, the wonder of being united with you. You are the source of all life and strength. In you is redemption, and we need to be redeemed before we can live rightly. Take from us the pressures forced on us by the flood of events. Make us completely free as people led by your hand, people who may be joyful because everything will be overcome through the power you grant us in Jesus Christ. Protect us from fear and from all evil. Show more and more clearly your good and wonderful goal for all people on earth, so that in expectation they may find happiness even in all the stress of today. Amen.

7
July

Let us hold unswervingly to the hope we profess, for he who promised is faithful. HEBREWS 10:23

Lord our God, we thank you for all you have done for us, for all you are doing for us, for deliverance from need and death. We thank you for all the signs you give us that you hear our prayer when, without wavering or weakening, we set our hopes on you. We thank you that we can be without fear of sin and death, for you stand by us in everything. In spite of our imperfections you show us your goodness again and again. May the light in our hearts never be extinguished, the light that enables us to look into heaven and earth and see the good that is on its way to us today. May joy remain with us, and may we have the strength to be a community that follows the paths of life which bring praise and honor to you. Amen.

8

July

The righteous cry out, and the Lord hears them; he delivers them from all their troubles. The Lord is close to the brokenhearted and saves those who are crushed in spirit. PSALM 34:17–18

Lord our God, our Father in heaven and on earth, we are thankful that you have a people to whom you say, "You are mine." Grant that we too may belong to this people. Strengthen us in the faith that we belong to you, so that we can come to know your rule and your justice. Protect us on all the paths we follow during our time on earth. The times are evil, but come what may, every single one of us has in his heart the certainty, "We are yours." You have long watched over us and kept us safe. Again and again we affirm, "We are yours, Lord our God, through Jesus Christ our Savior." Amen.

9
July

For this reason I kneel before the Father, from whom every family in heaven and on earth derives its name. I pray that out of his glorious riches he may strengthen you with power through his Spirit in your inner being, so that Christ may dwell in your hearts through faith.

EPHESIANS 3:14–17A

Lord our God, you are our Father, and we human beings know that our innermost hearts belong to you. Hold us firmly through your Spirit, we pray, so that we do not live on the level of our lower natures but remain true to the calling you have given us, the high calling to what is eternal. May all our experiences work in us for good, bringing us the joyful certainty that you rule us with your Spirit, that you further the good everywhere in the world and make more and more people sensitive to what is good, right, and perfect. Amen.

10

July

Come, let us bow down in worship, let us kneel before the Lord our Maker; for he is our God and we are the people of his pasture, the flock under his care. PSALM 95:6–7

Lord our God, strengthen in us all that comes from you and is eternal, all that is good and right and genuine. Let this shape our outward life and help us triumph over need and death. Help us to wait quietly, even when we don't know the answers to our questions, because we are certain that the outcome will be good and life-giving, to the glory of your Spirit and your name. We entrust ourselves to your hands. Stay with us, that we may receive your calling for our lives. Stay with us, so that in all our work and activity we may be aware of your guiding Spirit at work in our hearts. Amen.

11

July

Let us draw near to God with a sincere heart and with the full assurance that faith brings, having our hearts sprinkled to cleanse us from a guilty conscience and having our bodies washed with pure water.

HEBREWS 10:22

Lord our God, grant us true unity with your Son Jesus Christ, so that his power can be revealed in us and we may find new life in which we can truly serve you. Protect us from all error. Be among us with your Spirit to make us people who are genuine. Let your will be carried out more and more in this age. Let your will again intervene so that a new creation may come, a new heaven and a new earth, as we have been promised. May your name be great among us, may your kingdom come and everything in heaven and on earth be done according to your will. Amen.

12

July

I have been crucified with Christ and I no longer live, but Christ lives in me. The life I now live in the body, I live by faith in the Son of God, who loved me and gave himself for me. GALATIANS 2:20

Almighty God, keep watch over us and lead us fully into the life of Jesus Christ. Let your Son Jesus Christ become truly living within us so that we may be full of joy because we belong to the realm of heaven and may live every day with faith in him. We thank you for all you have let us experience. We thank you with all our hearts that in your great compassion you have showered so much good on us who are not yet perfect in faith. Keep our hearts in the light, we pray. Keep us patient and dedicated, for then more and more can be done among us poor children of earth, to the glory of your name. Amen.

13
July

Dear friends, now we are children of God, and what we will be has not yet been made known. But we know that when Christ appears, we shall be like him, for we shall see him as he is. 1 JOHN 3:2

Lord our mighty God, look upon us in our poverty, for you call us your children and give us of your Spirit. From your fullness we constantly need to receive strength for the struggle meant for us in life. Grant that light may come wherever darkness still reigns, especially where it is so black that we do not know which way to turn. Hear our prayer for all people, and let your justice and your truth alone be victorious. Let all people receive what you have promised them, and let them realize that no matter what happens, they remain your children. Amen.

14
July

"In that day I will respond," declares the Lord – "I will respond to the skies, and they will respond to the earth; and the earth will respond to the grain, the new wine and the olive oil, and they will respond to Jezreel. I will plant her for myself in the land; I will show my love to the one I called 'Not my loved one.' I will say to those called 'Not my people,' 'You are my people'; and they will say, 'You are my God.'" HOSEA 2:21–23

Lord our God, kindle true light in our hearts and minds, that we may recognize what we are and become free of everything false and dishonest. Let this light of righteousness, this judgment, go through all nations, that people no longer use empty words when they talk of "mercy" and "truth." Grant that your mercy and your truth find the right soil and bear fruit. May they find soil prepared by you, for you judge us and make right what is wrong in our earthly life. We thank you that however painful many of our experiences are, we may still say, "Through how much need has not our merciful God spread out his wings to protect us!" Amen.

15

July

I delight greatly in the Lord; my soul rejoices in my God. For he has clothed me with garments of salvation and arrayed me in a robe of his righteousness, as a bridegroom adorns his head like a priest, and as a bride adorns herself with her jewels. ISAIAH 61:10

Lord our God, grant that we may find the power of your Spirit so that we may live on a higher level, no longer controlled by our lower natures but strengthened to take up the battle of life. May we be children of the Spirit and may we walk in the Spirit. Guard us against carelessness and keep us joyful and courageous. Help us and counsel us on all our ways so that we may honor you and testify that you are our God, our true help. Amen.

16

July

But as for me, I watch in hope for the Lord, I wait for God my Savior; my God will hear me. Do not gloat over me, my enemy! Though I have fallen, I will rise. Though I sit in darkness, the Lord will be my light. MICAH 7:7–8

Dear Father in heaven, as your children we stand before you and lift our eyes to you. We are poor, needy people, often wretched and tormented. Let your eyes rest upon us. Grant us the help we need. Bless us when we gather in the name of Jesus Christ, that we may be a people who learn to serve you on all the paths we follow, even if it proves bitterly hard. Give us true faith for every moment. May we have joy and confidence that you are with your children, that you remain with them forever, until the great time of redemption when we will rejoice with all past generations and with all who are living today. Amen.

17

July

The Spirit of the Sovereign Lord is on me, because the Lord has anointed me to proclaim good news to the poor. He has sent me to bind up the brokenhearted, to proclaim freedom for the captives and release from darkness for the prisoners, to proclaim the year of the Lord's favor and the day of vengeance of our God, to comfort all who mourn.

ISAIAH 61:1–2

Lord our God, light of humankind in Jesus Christ, full of joy and trust we ask that we may have access to your almighty power, your power against all darkness, sin, death, and bondage. May we feel close to your almighty power. Hear our weeping, for we are and remain your children, to whom you have promised redemption and deliverance. Together we hold fast to this promise and stand before you saying, "We are your children in Jesus Christ the Savior, whom you have sent to us." Hear your children. Bless us each one, and bless us as one people, allowed to serve you in the misery of our world. Amen.

18

July

Yet a time is coming and has now come when the true worshipers will worship the Father in the Spirit and in truth, for they are the kind of worshipers the Father seeks. God is spirit, and his worshipers must worship in the Spirit and in truth. JOHN 4:23–24

Lord our God, we thank you for being among us as our Father, for letting us be your children on earth. We thank you that as your children we can find life in spirit and in truth. Grant that each of us may find how our lives on earth can be lifted up by your Spirit. Your Spirit can bring us what we do not possess, so that our daily work, all our striving and struggling for the outward things of life, may be pervaded by what is higher and greater. Your Spirit can keep us from falling into base and petty ways, from getting lost in earthly experiences which do not last, no matter how much they demand our attention. We thank you for all you have done for your children. Continue to help us, that we may serve you every day in gladness and gratitude. Amen.

19

July

But he said to me, "My grace is sufficient for you, for my power is made perfect in weakness." Therefore I will boast all the more gladly about my weaknesses, so that Christ's power may rest on me. That is why, for Christ's sake, I delight in weaknesses, in insults, in hardships, in persecutions, in difficulties. For when I am weak, then I am strong. 2 CORINTHIANS 12:9–10

Lord our God, we rejoice that we may be called your children. In our weakness we ask you to shelter us in your hands. Strengthen us in the hope and faith that our lives will surely go the right way, not through our strength but through your protection. Grant that through your Spirit we may come to know more and more that you are with us. Help us to be alert in our daily life and to listen whenever you want to say something to us. Reveal the power and glory of your kingdom in many people, to the glory of your name, and hasten the coming on earth of all that is good and true. Amen.

20
July

They will be my people, and I will be their God. I will give them singleness of heart and action, so that they will always fear me and that all will then go well for them and for their children after them. JEREMIAH 32:38–39

Lord our God, you want to be our God and you want us to be your people. Give us the inner integrity and the power to discern and reject what does not come from the heart, so that everything may be genuine among us. Then no lies and deception will creep in, and honesty and goodness will flow from our hearts to the glory of truth, to the glory of the gospel and the great hope you give through the gospel. Guard our hearts. Protect the good that is planted in them, that it may grow and thrive and bear fruit. Amen.

21

July

My soul yearns, even faints, for the courts of the Lord; my heart and my flesh cry out for the living God. Even the sparrow has found a home, and the swallow a nest for herself, where she may have her young – a place near your altar, Lord Almighty, my King and my God. Blessed are those who dwell in your house; they are ever praising you. PSALM 84:2–4

Lord God, our souls long for you and for your glory, for the day when it shall be said, "All is accomplished! Now your kingdom comes. Now your day appears. When we look back on all that has happened to us, everything becomes clear." We thank you that we can live without fear, again and again refreshed and renewed, waiting for the good you give on earth. Show us the way we have to go. Grant your blessing in our hearts so that in need and death, in fear and distress, we may always have light and strength. You are our salvation, Lord our God. From you comes the salvation of our souls. We trust you today and every day. We praise your name, and in you we hope for the day you hold in readiness for the whole world, the day when light will dawn in every heart. Amen.

22

July

You are those who have stood by me in my trials. And I confer on you a kingdom, just as my Father conferred one on me, so that you may eat and drink at my table in my kingdom. LUKE 22:28–30A

Lord our God, we thank you that we may be your children and that we may hope in your Spirit. Your Spirit rules us as people whom you want to draw to yourself, as people who may serve you in their lives here on earth. Grant that we may be childlike, so that your Spirit can rule us more and more and what is good may come to many people in all places. May many come to know that their lives are not merely temporal. May they realize that they can live and act in you, and through you may experience the good that is to come to all nations on earth. Amen.

23
July

Salvation is found in no one else, for there is no other name under heaven given to mankind by which we must be saved. ACTS 4:12

Dear Father in heaven, we thank you that you have revealed to us the name Jesus Christ, the name of your Son, who leads us to you as your children. May your hand be plainly seen over all the suffering and dying people of our time. May your hand soon bring in a new age, a time truly of God and of the Savior, fulfilling what has long been promised. Watch over us this night. Bless us. In suffering, continue to uphold us with your mighty hand. In grief, may your name still be honored. May your kingdom come, breaking into all the evil of the world, and may your will be done on earth as in heaven. Amen.

24
July

So do not throw away your confidence; it will be richly rewarded. You need to persevere so that when you have done the will of God, you will receive what he has promised. HEBREWS 10:35–36

Lord our God, we bow down before you in this time when you have brought us hardships and judgment. Change this earthly age, we beseech you. Bring in something from heaven so that your will may be done and your mercy come to all nations. Strengthen us on all our ways, we pray. We thank you for all you have done for us. May your name be praised and glorified at all times. We want to follow you and to remain in your heavenly life. Amen.

25

July

May the favor of the Lord our God rest on us; establish the work of our hands for us – yes, establish the work of our hands. PSALM 90:17

Dear Father in heaven, Creator of what is good, beautiful, and full of joy so that all may work in harmony with you, we thank you for all the good that comes to us. May we be your children, joined together to serve you. May our life bring joy to others, and may we do good without ceasing through your great, strong love, which moves us, strengthens us, and helps us every day, however hard life may be. May your name be praised throughout the world. May your kingdom come and your will be done on earth as in heaven. Amen.

26

July

Your word, Lord, is eternal; it stands firm in the heavens. Your faithfulness continues through all generations; you established the earth, and it endures. Your laws endure to this day, for all things serve you. PSALM 119:89–91

Lord God, we thank you for your Word, greatest and most glorious of all that comes to our human life. Every day we want to find more joy in your help, in what you are doing for us. Again and again we feel and rejoice in the new help, new strength, and new courage for life given by your Word. We seek and seek to find Jesus Christ, the eternal Life. He will surely come to establish your kingdom. Praise to your name, eternal, glorious, almighty God! Be with us poor, lowly people. Strengthen us in spirit, and enable us to persevere until everything is fulfilled that is promised by your Word. Amen.

27

July

I have other sheep that are not of this sheep pen. I must bring them also. They too will listen to my voice, and there shall be one flock and one shepherd. JOHN 10:16

Lord our God, bring us together as one. Give us your Spirit so that we may know you, so that joy may fill our hearts, not only for ourselves but also for others. Root out evil from the earth. Sweep away all that offends you, all lying, deceit, and hate between nations. Grant that all people may come to know you, so that disunity and conflict may be swept away and your eternal kingdom may arise on earth and we may rejoice in it. For your kingdom can come to people even while on earth to bring them happiness and to make them your own children. Yes, Lord God, we want to be your children, your people, held in your hand, so that your name may be honored, your kingdom may come, and your will be done on earth as in heaven. Amen.

28

July

The law was brought in so that the trespass might increase. But where sin increased, grace increased all the more, so that, just as sin reigned in death, so also grace might reign through righteousness to bring eternal life through Jesus Christ our Lord. ROMANS 5:20–21

Lord our God, we come into your presence, pleading with you to bring the world what it needs, so that people may be freed from all their pain and enabled to serve you. Let the power of Jesus Christ be revealed in our time. For he has taken on our sin that justice might arise on earth, that all might have life and might see your salvation, which you will bring when the time is fulfilled. Let your power be revealed in the world, and let your will be done, your name be kept holy, and all wrongs be righted in this turbulent and difficult age. O Lord our God, you alone can help. You alone are the Savior of all peoples. In your great mercy you can bring peace. We look to you. And when we consider your Word, we remember the mighty promises you have given, promises which are to be fulfilled in our time. Amen.

29

July

On my return I will not spare those who sinned earlier or any of the others, since you are demanding proof that Christ is speaking through me. He is not weak in dealing with you, but is powerful among you. For to be sure, he was crucified in weakness, yet he lives by God's power. Likewise, we are weak in him, yet by God's power we will live with him in our dealing with you.

2 CORINTHIANS 13:2B–4

Lord our God, we thank you for the love you show us so that we may be delivered from weakness and sickness, from sin and misery, and may be given strength to serve you, our Father in heaven. Bless us in all we have on our hearts, that through your mercy the battle of life may be fought aright. Bless us in our times and grant that justice may gain the upper hand and we may live in peace, praising you into all eternity. Protect us, your children, forevermore. May your name be honored, your kingdom come, and your will be done on earth as in heaven. Amen.

30

July

For the Spirit God gave us does not make us timid, but gives us power, love and self-discipline. 2 TIMOTHY 1:7

Lord our God, we are your children. Hear all our concerns, we pray, for we want help from you, not from men, not from anything we can think or say. May your power be revealed in our time. We long for a new age, an age of peace in which people are changed. We long for your day, the day when your power will be revealed to poor, broken humankind. Be with us, and give our hearts what will remain with us, the strength and mercy of Jesus Christ. Amen.

31

July

There are many who say, "O that we might see some good! Let the light of your face shine on us, O Lord!"

PSALM 4:6, NRSV

Lord our God, with all our hearts we come before your countenance. Our hearts shall always be in your presence, asking, longing, and believing that you will guide our affairs aright. Protect us, for you are our God and Father. Protect all who are in danger or who must go into danger. Make known your great love and your living presence to the hearts of the dying. Draw our hearts together so that we may have community in you, our faith and hope set on you alone. Protect us during the night, and help us to be at peace about all our concerns because they are in your hands. Every concern of every person is in your hands. We ourselves are in your hands, Lord God, our Father, and there we want to remain. Your hands can heal and restore everything. Praised be your name! Amen.

August

1

August

However, as it is written: "What no eye has seen, what no ear has heard, and what no human mind has conceived" – the things God has prepared for those who love him" – these are the things God has revealed to us by his Spirit. 1 CORINTHIANS 2:9–10A

Lord our God, bless us all through your Spirit, that we may find certainty of heart in community with you under your rulership. May we keep this certainty, whatever course our lives may take, whatever battles and suffering may come to us, for we belong to you and you rule and guide us as your children. Watch over all who are still far away from you but who long for you. Watch over all who are good-hearted and sincere, even if they often do not understand you. Protect them, and let your kingdom come so that your will is carried out more and more by the many who feel compelled to seek for you and for the goodness and truth which are your will. May we and many others serve you with our whole lives. Amen.

2
August

Rejoice always, pray continually, give thanks in all circumstances; for this is God's will for you in Christ Jesus. I THESSALONIANS 5:16–18

Father in heaven, we thank you that we may feel your leading, your lordship, for you have blessed us with every spiritual and heavenly gift in Christ. We thank you that we may be among those who receive true life always anew, who praise and glorify you, exulting even in difficult days. For it is just in the difficult days that we need to belong to those who are thankful and joyful, who always find new certainty in their lives. With them may we experience the good you give on earth so that humankind may be blest and come at last into your hands. Amen.

3
August

The true light that gives light to everyone was coming into the world. He was in the world, and though the world was made through him, the world did not recognize him. He came to that which was his own, but his own did not receive him. Yet to all who did receive him, to those who believed in his name, he gave the right to become children of God. JOHN 1:9–12

Dear Father in heaven, we thank you that we may be your children. We thank you for giving us your Spirit so that we may truly be your children. Gather us into community with you so that our minds and hearts and all that is in us may realize what joy can come to us through your gifts. Though the world today is in turmoil, in doubt, lost in material things, grant us inner quiet to receive from you the power of faith. For through faith we can learn to know what you are and what you will be to all humankind one day, through Jesus Christ the Lord. Amen.

4

August

As a prisoner for the Lord, then, I urge you to live a life worthy of the calling you have received. Be completely humble and gentle; be patient, bearing with one another in love. Make every effort to keep the unity of the Spirit through the bond of peace. EPHESIANS 4:1–3

Dear Father in heaven, we thank you for the blessings you give us on earth, for it is through your gifts and work, and through the work of your children, that we can believe and be saved. Protect us here in our household. Let us make allowances for one another in love and spare no effort to maintain unity in the Spirit through the bond of peace. Grant us new strength and new gifts whenever we need them on the path you have set for us. Grant that we may rejoice and trust in you until we reach the goal. Amen.

5

August

Simon Peter answered him, "Lord, to whom shall we go? You have the words of eternal life. We have come to believe and to know that you are the Holy One of God."

JOHN 6:68–69

Dear Father in heaven, we come to you and seek communion with you because we know that all life comes from you, all progress among us depends on you, and our innermost being can be strengthened through your Spirit. Protect us and renew our strength time and again so that your will may be done among us and we may all find courage for our lives, even when many difficulties loom up around us. Grant that we may remain your servants and go joyfully to meet what is to come. Bless us today and every day according to your promises. Amen.

6

August

I have swept away your offenses like a cloud, your sins like the morning mist. Return to me, for I have redeemed you. ISAIAH 44:22

Lord our God, we thank you for establishing us on the firm foundation of your Word and your promise, your promise that expresses the great longing and hope in so many people's hearts. For they do not want their lives to remain base and petty but want to look toward something higher, rejoicing that the promise can be fulfilled for them. So today we too stand ready for the coming time you are bringing, and we exult in our expectation of the future. We rejoice in the expectation of the time when you will give your Spirit to us and to all those who answer your call and become your helpers. Amen.

7
August

Believe in the light while you have the light, so that you may become children of light. JOHN 12:36

Dear Father in heaven, as your children we come into your presence so that you may lead us with the light that streams out from you. We come to your light seeking an inner birth to make us what your children ought to be. Bless us as we thank you for all your goodness and for the powerful help you have given many among us. Accept the thanks we offer you, and grant that we never forget the good you are doing for us. Help us to go forward, always forward, until your kingdom is completed. May it not be in vain that we live in the Lord Jesus and in love to you, the God and Father of all. May it not be in vain that we bring you our requests and prayers for your kingdom to come soon. Yes, Lord Jesus, come! Come soon to this earth so that all people may acknowledge the true God and may love you. Amen.

8

August

Do nothing from selfish ambition or conceit, but in humility regard others as better than yourselves. Let each of you look not to your own interests, but to the interests of others. Let the same mind be in you that was in Christ Jesus. PHILIPPIANS 2:3–5, NRSV

Lord our God, we come before you in the great name of Jesus Christ. We thank you that while we are still living on earth you give us hope and joy in this great name. May something be born in us through your Spirit to make us of one mind with Jesus Christ. In all our relationships with others may we learn that it is better to submit in patience than to dominate, better to serve than to rule, better to be the weakest than to bring pressure to bear on others. Give us this attitude. Let this attitude arise in many so that they may be Christians not only in their words and thoughts, but Christians at heart, loving their neighbors and at one with the Savior on every step of the way. Amen.

9

August

For where two or three gather in my name, there am I with them. MATTHEW 18:20

Lord our God and our Father, we praise you because we are allowed to have community together in the name of Jesus, who has opened our eyes to see you and who has promised to be among us when we are gathered in his name. May our hearts remain unshadowed, even when our lives seem to grow difficult and the future looks dark. Protect us whenever we are tempted and have battles to fight. Deliver us. Make us free people who know we belong to you and who are allowed while still on earth to have a share in eternal life. Amen.

10

August

Who shall separate us from the love of Christ? Shall trouble or hardship or persecution or famine or nakedness or danger or sword?...No, in all these things we are more than conquerors through him who loved us.

ROMANS 8:35, 37

Lord our God! What can separate us from your love? Can trouble or fear or persecution or hunger or nakedness or peril or the sword? In all these things we are more than conquerors through him who loved us. Dear Father in heaven, we long for courage. You will answer our prayers and again and again grant us strength, the power of your Spirit, the only power that can strengthen us. We thank you for all you have done for us. Help us onward from victory to victory until everything on earth is won for the good, to your honor among all humankind. Amen.

11

August

How beautiful on the mountains are the feet of those who bring good news, who proclaim peace, who bring good tidings, who proclaim salvation, who say to Zion, "Your God reigns!" Listen! Your watchmen lift up their voices; together they shout for joy. When the Lord returns to Zion, they will see it with their own eyes. ISAIAH 52:7–8

Lord our God, grant that we may be your watchmen, who understand what you mean for our time. We thank you for all you have already done, for every change to the good among the nations. For the nations must bow to your will; nothing happens unless accomplished by you. Judge us wherever necessary. Open our eyes to see where we are wrong and not in accord with your Spirit. Be with us and give us strength. Wherever something happens to move people's hearts, let the watchmen proclaim, "This comes from God. It does not matter how much we suffer. This comes from Jesus Christ, who suffered and died, but who rose again." Raise up such watchmen among young and old everywhere on earth. Let there be a people who go to meet you with shouts of joy and thanksgiving. Amen.

12

August

The Lord is my strength and my shield; my heart trusts in him, and he helps me. My heart leaps for joy, and with my song I praise him. PSALM 28:7

Lord our God, you are our strength and shield. Our hearts hope in you and we are helped. Accept us from among all the nations as a people who want to serve you. Strengthen our hearts, especially when we must be tested in every way and must face the many hardships that will come when we take up our task of proclaiming your name and witnessing to you. For you are strong and can protect us. You can fill us with light and with joy to proclaim again and again the salvation that is coming through your all-powerful goodness and mercy, salvation in Jesus Christ the Lord. Amen.

13
August

Those the Lord has rescued will return. They will enter Zion with singing; everlasting joy will crown their heads. Gladness and joy will overtake them, and sorrow and sighing will flee away. "I, even I, am he who comforts you." ISAIAH 51:11–12A

Lord our God, we thank you for the trust you have put into our hearts. We thank you for all the signs of your goodness that comfort us when we are in great need and when many deaths take place around us and touch each of us. We thank you for comforting us, for always giving us fresh courage wherever we may be, and for giving us hope for other people, who also struggle hard to find what is good. O Lord God, bless our world with power from on high, with your gifts that bring good to many people. Bless our world. Save it from sin, from ruin, from every kind of despair. Give your blessing, O Lord our God! As you bless us, so bless all the world, to the glory of your name. Amen.

14
August

If only you had paid attention to my commands, your peace would have been like a river, your well-being like the waves of the sea. ISAIAH 48:18

Lord our God, help us to heed your commandments, that our peace may be like a river and our righteousness like the waves of the sea. Be with us through your Spirit, we pray. Speak with us and tell us what we need to hear so that we can understand what draws us always nearer to you. Show the might of your hand to help us and all people. Even under judgment we shall not despair, we shall not lose courage because of troubles and distress. Come with your strength, that we may grow strong to overcome the world through Jesus Christ the Savior. Amen.

15
August

We always thank God, the Father of our Lord Jesus Christ, when we pray for you, because we have heard of your faith in Christ Jesus and of the love you have for all God's people – the faith and love that spring from the hope stored up for you in heaven and about which you have already heard in the true message of the gospel that has come to you. In the same way, the gospel is bearing fruit and growing throughout the whole world – just as it has been doing among you since the day you heard it and truly understood God's grace. COLOSSIANS 1:3–6

Lord our God, we praise your name because we are allowed to bear witness to what we see and hear, to all the good you have given us. May we become firmly and faithfully united, awaiting the glorious day when your almighty hand will be victorious and will bring an end to the many evils among us. On that day you will be praised throughout all nations and everything will be clothed anew, to the glory of your great name. Amen.

16

August

Trust in him, and he will help you; make your ways straight, and hope in him. You who fear the Lord, wait for his mercy; do not stray, or else you may fall. You who fear the Lord, trust in him, and your reward will not be lost.

ECCLESIASTICUS 2:6–8, NRSV

Dear Father in heaven, we come before you to receive what we need as your children who cannot find help and guidance on our own, but only through your Spirit. Enlighten us by your Word, which you alone can give. You will give us your Word so that we can know with absolute certainty and clarity how to serve you. Your Word will show us the truth that is to be revealed on earth in Jesus Christ. Shelter us in your hands. Strengthen us especially during suffering, and free us from fear and trembling. Fill our hearts with patience and joy. Amen.

17
August

Peace I leave with you; my peace I give you. I do not give to you as the world gives. Do not let your hearts be troubled and do not be afraid. JOHN 14:27

Dear Father in heaven, we thank you for holding open the way into our hearts and for bringing us the peace of Jesus Christ. Help us to keep this way open. Grant us peace in this tempest-torn world. Grant us peace when many struggles and uncertainties try to occupy our hearts. We have no strength in ourselves, only in him who is standing at our side and who will never forsake us, who lives and gives strength. His light will always break in anew among us. His light will shine on many people and lead them to the promised day, the day that will bring all our hopes to fulfillment. Amen.

18

August

Yet I am always with you; you hold me by my right hand. You guide me with your counsel, and afterward you will take me into glory. PSALM 73:23–24

Thank you, great God and Father, for filling our hearts with trust so that we are of good hope, also for those who have not yet found trust. Thank you for giving us courage to face all the questions that arise in human life and for accepting us again and again when we come to you. You know what lies before us. You know the mountains that have to be moved. You know all the things that frustrate us and try to wear us out, and you will take them away. At last your light will shine into all the darkness. This certainty fills us with gladness and thanksgiving. In this faith we are determined to remain steadfast and to press on to victory. Amen.

19

August

Whom have I in heaven but you? And earth has nothing I desire besides you. My flesh and my heart may fail, but God is the strength of my heart and my portion forever.

PSALM 73:25–26

Dear God and our Father, if only we have you, we desire nothing more in heaven or on earth. Body and soul may fail, but you, O God, are the strength and comfort of our hearts and you are ours forever. May we live in your Spirit and may your light shine over us. Touch our hearts and help us understand the greatness of what you call us to. Help us and free us again and again so that we are not bound by fear, even when we must pass through intense suffering. For your hand shall be with us and shall rescue us. Your hand shall bring about good for us and for all the people around us. Our hearts go out to them and we plead for them too, "Lord, send your Savior to all." Amen.

20

August

Therefore, there is now no condemnation for those who are in Christ Jesus. ROMANS 8:1

Lord our God, grant that we may be your children who receive the Spirit and all they need from you. You strengthen us not only physically but also inwardly, in our hearts, enabling us to face the uncertainties of earthly life and whatever still needs changing in human society. Keep us from giving in to weakness. May your power be always with us. May we have patience and hope, because you are working for the good and we may wait for it in expectation. Amen.

21
August

Finally, brothers and sisters, whatever is true, whatever is noble, whatever is right, whatever is pure, whatever is lovely, whatever is admirable – if anything is excellent or praiseworthy – think about such things. Whatever you have learned or received or heard from me, or seen in me – put it into practice. And the God of peace will be with you. PHILIPPIANS 4:8–9

Dear Father in heaven, let our thoughts be filled with all that is honorable, just, pure, gracious, good, and praiseworthy. We want to await your Spirit, not giving way to anxiety, but showing ourselves worthy to be your children. We want to be your children, who can rise above even the most difficult conditions and maintain a quiet trust, to the glory of your Spirit within us. Protect us now and always in your divine peace. Amen.

22
August

As the deer pants for streams of water, so my soul pants for you, my God. My soul thirsts for God, for the living God. When can I go and meet with God?...Why, my soul, are you downcast? Why so disturbed within me? Put your hope in God, for I will yet praise him, my Savior and my God. PSALM 42: 1–2, 5

Lord our God, as the deer pants for refreshing water, so our souls long for you, O God. Our souls thirst for you, for the living God. We stand in your presence and pour out our hearts to you. We bring before you everything that is painful to us, all our suffering and needs. We also bring you all our hopes and the many proofs you have given us that our lives need not go to ruin but can be directed to greater things. May the light of your Spirit shine on us today and always. Amen.

23

August

Therefore, my brothers and sisters, make every effort to confirm your calling and election. For if you do these things, you will never stumble, and you will receive a rich welcome into the eternal kingdom of our Lord and Savior Jesus Christ. 2 PETER 1:10–11

Lord our God, we thank you that you have given us an entrance into the eternal kingdom of our Lord and Savior Jesus Christ. We thank you that you have already begun to give us new vision, that already many things are being transformed, so that we may go gladly and confidently on our way with hope for whatever is still unsolved. May all this live in our hearts and fill us with thanks to you. We want to be courageous and keep in sight what still needs to be changed. Then we can take part as workers in your vineyard. May the light you have given us continue to shine in us and burn ever more brightly, as you have promised. Amen.

24
August

In addition to all this, take up the shield of faith, with which you can extinguish all the flaming arrows of the evil one. EPHESIANS 6:16

Lord our God, we long to come into your light, to live in your strength, that we may do what pleases you and furthers your kingdom on earth. Protect us from evil and do not let us be wounded by the flaming arrows of the evil one. Make paths for us whenever we do not know how to go forward. We always know you are our Father. Because you are our Father, we want to be courageous and persevere to the end so that you can make our lives bear fruit for you, to the glory of your name. Amen.

25
August

Do not conform to the pattern of this world, but be transformed by the renewing of your mind. Then you will be able to test and approve what God's will is – his good, pleasing and perfect will. ROMANS 12:2

Grant us your Spirit, Lord our God, that we may discern your good, acceptable, and perfect will. Give us joy in fighting on your side, so that what is good, acceptable, and perfect may be given to the world. Wherever we are and whatever work we do, give us zeal to serve you and be guided by you so that your will may be done and your kingdom come, so that already today we may find happiness even though only in hope. Amen.

26

August

Show me your ways, Lord, teach me your paths. Guide me in your truth and teach me, for you are God my Savior, and my hope is in you all day long. PSALM 25:4–5

Lord our God, be our Father and care for your children here on earth, where it is often bitterly hard and where everything seems to turn against us. Keep us faithful in our inner life, drawing all our strength from you, the eternal power of life, and from Jesus Christ, the Savior of the world. For Jesus has promised to come to us, and you will send him in our time of need. Let your strong hand be with those who often do not know where to turn. Show us paths we can follow, to the glory of your name in all eternity. Amen.

27

August

Hear my voice when I call, Lord; be merciful to me and answer me. My heart says of you, "Seek his face!" Your face, Lord, I will seek. Do not hide your face from me.

PSALM 27:7–9A

We thank you, dear Father in heaven, that you let the light from your face shine into our hearts. Look upon our time, we pray, with your clear, penetrating eyes, and let all people sense that they are watched over by more than they are able to see. Let them realize that a strong God and Father is watching over them. Protect us on our way, and let your light shine ever more brightly, so that in all we do your name is glorified. Amen.

28

August

The Lord reigns, he is robed in majesty; the Lord is robed in majesty and armed with strength; indeed, the world is established, firm and secure. PSALM 93:1

Lord our God, you are king, founding a kingdom that reaches to the ends of the earth, establishing it to endure forever. We thank you that we may be sheltered in your hands and that no sickness of body or soul can do us lasting harm. We thank you for lifting us again and again to true life with the light and power to overcome what is earthly, true life with the flexibility to remain trusting and confident no matter what happens, true life directed to the great goal of God's kingdom, promised to us in Jesus Christ. Amen.

29
August

Remember your leaders, who spoke the word of God to you. Consider the outcome of their way of life and imitate their faith...Do not be carried away by all kinds of strange teachings. It is good for our hearts to be strengthened by grace, not by eating ceremonial foods, which is of no benefit to those who do so. HEBREWS 13:7, 9

Lord our God, dear Father in heaven, we thank you for all you do in our lives, for you stretch out your hand to us on earth through our Savior Jesus Christ. We entrust ourselves to you, knowing that everything depends on your rule over our lives. It is your rule that enables us to go forward in your strength and in your light, always finding new joy in spite of struggles and temptations. May your mighty hand be with those who call to you, no matter how they may do it. You see into their hearts. You know those who are sincere, and you will send your Savior to bring them out of all evil and darkness. Be with us today and every day. Amen.

30
August

My sheep listen to my voice; I know them, and they follow me. I give them eternal life, and they shall never perish; no one will snatch them out of my hand.

JOHN 10:27–28

Dear Father in heaven, we thank you for moving our hearts so that we may know we are your children. Even in the midst of turmoil and evil, fear and pain, you bring us happiness; we can know that you are holding us with your right hand and will finally deliver us from all evil. Let your Spirit be at work everywhere. Give us patience when time is needed in our own hearts and in the hearts of all people, who also belong to you. Continue to strengthen us so that even the heaviest burden does not crush us and we may exult in hope because you right every wrong, to the glory of your name. Amen.

31

August

This, then, is how you ought to regard us: as servants of Christ and as those entrusted with the mysteries God has revealed. Now it is required that those who have been given a trust must prove faithful. 1 CORINTHIANS 4:1–2

Dear Father in heaven, open our hearts to see and feel how our lives have been blest. Open our hearts to your blessings so that we may look forward in thankfulness and joy to what lies ahead. Grant that we may be faithful to what we have received from you and never again lose ourselves in the passing moment. May we hold to all you have brought to our hearts from eternity, that your name may be honored and our lives shaped anew in Jesus Christ. Give us courage to overcome the evils in life and to look with joy and confident expectation to the future, when the powers of your kingdom will be ever more clearly revealed. Amen.

September

1

September

Therefore, if anyone is in Christ, the new creation has come: The old has gone, the new is here!

2 CORINTHIANS 5:17

Dear Father in heaven, open our hearts to see what is good in our lives. May the light in our hearts shine clearly so that we see, recognize, and live in accordance with what comes from eternity and belongs to our true nature, brought to us through Christ. Keep us from being blinded and deafened by experiences that will pass by. Help us to rise above them even in suffering and to wait patiently for what is becoming new and perfect. Praise to your name that we too can say, "The old has passed away; see, everything has become new!" Amen.

2
September

Rather, as servants of God we commend ourselves in every way: in great endurance; in troubles, hardships and distresses; in beatings, imprisonments and riots; in hard work, sleepless nights and hunger...through glory and dishonor, bad report and good report; genuine, yet regarded as impostors; known, yet regarded as unknown; dying, and yet we live on; beaten, and yet not killed; sorrowful, yet always rejoicing; poor, yet making many rich; having nothing, and yet possessing everything.

2 CORINTHIANS 6:4–5, 8–10

Dear Father in heaven, you are always near to us on earth, and we thank you for all the love you put into our lives so that we can be joyful, even in all kinds of temptations and struggles. How much you have given us and how often you have rescued us from distress! Again and again you have let the light of life shine out. You give us light not only for the moment but also for the future, enabling us to draw strength and assurance from the present, the past, and the future, to the glory of your name. Amen.

3
September

Therefore we do not lose heart. Though outwardly we are wasting away, yet inwardly we are being renewed day by day. For our light and momentary troubles are achieving for us an eternal glory that far outweighs them all. So we fix our eyes not on what is seen, but on what is unseen, since what is seen is temporary, but what is unseen is eternal. 2 CORINTHIANS 4:16–18

Lord our God, we thank you that you come to help us with your power and might. We thank you that you come to us in our suffering and strengthen us in all we must endure on earth. You help us so that what is good and full of light comes more and more to us and to all people. We thank you and pray that your power, coming from the invisible world into the visible, may continue its quiet working in us until the day when everyone can see Jesus Christ, who is the same yesterday, today, and into all eternity. Amen.

4
September

He saved us, not because of righteous things we had done, but because of his mercy. He saved us through the washing of rebirth and renewal by the Holy Spirit, whom he poured out on us generously through Jesus Christ our Savior, so that, having been justified by his grace, we might become heirs having the hope of eternal life.

TITUS 3:5–7

Lord our God, let your light shine in our hearts, the light that can gladden us and lead us until all our longing is stilled. May the higher nature born in us become ever stronger so that the lower and perishable nature does not rule over us. Grant that we may overcome and that our hearts may rejoice in being allowed to strive for the highest good because we are your children who can share in what is eternal. Amen.

5
September

I have fought the good fight, I have finished the race, I have kept the faith. Now there is in store for me the crown of righteousness, which the Lord, the righteous Judge, will award to me on that day – and not only to me, but also to all who have longed for his appearing.

2 TIMOTHY 4:7–8

We thank you, Father in heaven, that you concern yourself with us and that you bind us to yourself through all your deeds and all your help. We thank you for showing us a way of hope, a way that becomes always clearer, always firmer under our feet. On this way we can defy every evil of this world and time, knowing for sure that everything will come out right and we will all be brought to the great, eternal goal, even though we have to deny ourselves and go through much suffering. Your kingdom must come to the glory of your name, so that all people may live on a higher plane and follow you, the only true help and true life. Amen.

6

September

When Jesus saw this, he was indignant. He said to them, "Let the little children come to me, and do not hinder them, for the kingdom of God belongs to such as these. Truly I tell you, anyone who will not receive the kingdom of God like a little child will never enter it."

MARK 10:14–15

Dear Father in heaven, how shall we thank you for all you give to us, your children – for the great wisdom and power you hold in readiness for us if we are child-like? We want to be glad in your presence. We do not want to weep and complain, though tears often threaten to come. We ask you to protect us, your children. Protect all your children on earth. Let the pain that breaks over them be taken away. Even when we must follow a hard road, let the suffering we endure become part of the fight that brings in the kingdom of heaven, bringing your purpose to the earth and your great mercy, the wonderful forgiveness that enables people to be reborn, until at last all are called your children. Sustain us. Help us. Bless us. May the Savior always live among us, reviving and strengthening us in body and soul. Amen.

7

September

Praise be to the God and Father of our Lord Jesus Christ! In his great mercy he has given us new birth into a living hope through the resurrection of Jesus Christ from the dead, and into an inheritance that can never perish, spoil or fade. This inheritance is kept in heaven for you.

I PETER 1:3–4

Lord our God, remind us again and again of what you have done in our hearts and lives to make us certain of the resurrection. Help us to live in this certainty and to hold fast to everything good and great which you bring into our lives. Grant us the assurance that we are gaining ground in the battle for the redemption of those who are still in darkness and in the shadow of death. May we find joy in what we have here and now. Give us patience in our struggles. Give us hope for all that has gone wrong, because even what is in darkness is still in your hands. In the end everything must be brought to the light so that all humankind may glorify your great name. Amen.

8

September

"Has God forgotten to be merciful? Has he in anger withheld his compassion?" Then I thought, "To this I will appeal: the years when the Most High stretched out his right hand. I will remember the deeds of the Lord; yes, I will remember your miracles of long ago. I will consider all your works and meditate on all your mighty deeds."

PSALM 77:9–12

Lord God, our Father in heaven, we turn to you in these times when we are under so much stress and temptation. Let your light glow in our hearts to give us firmness, patience, and perseverance throughout the time of testing, no matter how long it lasts. Your hand can change everything. Your hand can shorten the time we must wait until your light shines out of the darkness of death and evil, until your light reveals your life to your children and to the whole world. You are our God and Father as you have promised, and remaining at your side, we look to you in faith and trust. You will bring about goodness, justice, and mercy as you have promised, and so fulfill your will. Amen.

9

September

Finally, be strong in the Lord and in his mighty power. Put on the full armor of God, so that you can take your stand against the devil's schemes. EPHESIANS 6:10–11

Lord God, we thank you that it is your will to strengthen us through your presence, through Jesus Christ, the leader of your cause, who is and remains victor among all on earth. Our souls need strength and our hearts need confidence so that in our time we can draw near to you and to your kingdom. Bless us with the Holy Spirit whenever we begin to grow weary. Your Holy Spirit can give us the strength to believe and hope, the strength to see the salvation that is coming to give joy to all the world. Amen.

10

September

Your word is a lamp for my feet, a light on my path.

PSALM 119:105

Lord our God, we stand before your presence. Look in mercy upon us poor, weak children, who do not know where to turn unless you help us with your mighty hand. We trust in you. You will help us, you will always be with us, and even in hard times you will accomplish your will for what is good. Bless us today as we gather to hear your Word. May your Word always be our strength and joy. Your Word gives victory in us and in the whole world so that your will may be done on earth as in heaven. Amen.

11

September

After he has suffered, he will see the light of life and be satisfied; by his knowledge my righteous servant will justify many, and he will bear their iniquities.

ISAIAH 53:11

Lord our God, our Father in heaven, we thank you for letting our failures and sins come before you and for giving us One who steps in to help us just as we are, with the right help for the good and the evil things in our lives. We thank you that our whole age can be comforted, and even the terrors of our days can be turned to the good because everything has already come before your holy eyes. Salvation will come out of disaster, life out of death. Praise to your glorious and almighty name! Protect our faith in your Servant. May we always find strength and courage, even when we are in pain. The time is coming when your loving-kindness will be revealed among all nations on earth. Amen.

12
September

When you hear of wars and rumors of wars, do not be alarmed. Such things must happen, but the end is still to come. Nation will rise against nation, and kingdom against kingdom. There will be earthquakes in various places, and famines. These are the beginning of birth pains...And the gospel must first be preached to all nations...Everyone will hate you because of me, but the one who stands firm to the end will be saved.

MARK 13:7–8,10, 13

Lord our God, Ruler over the world, whose longing is to see your thoughts and your will in all peoples, we come before you and ask that we may find strength in your Word and never cease to hope for the coming of your kingdom. Even when the world storms and rages, even when earthly kingdoms rise up against each other and everything seems dark, even then be present. Let your kingdom go quietly forward, to the honor of your name. Help us come closer to the goal Jesus has shown us, closer to the time we wait for, the day of his coming when all shall be made new and good through your power, through your Spirit. Amen.

13

September

For it is by grace you have been saved, through faith – and this is not from yourselves, it is the gift of God – not by works, so that no one can boast. EPHESIANS 2:8–9

Lord our God, we know that we are your children, and in this certainty we gather in your presence as a community. Grant us your Spirit, the Spirit who works in us and frees us from the many evils that still torment us. Be with us and let the power of your great grace and mercy be in our hearts so that we may gain the victory and lead joyful lives on earth in spite of our many shortcomings, blunders, and sins. For your grace is great, much greater than all our failings. You are our God and Father, and we want to keep our consciences clear today and always through your grace. Amen.

14

September

"This is the covenant I will make with the people of Israel after that time," declares the Lord. "I will put my law in their minds and write it on their hearts. I will be their God, and they will be my people. No longer will they teach their neighbor, or say to one another, 'Know the Lord,' because they will all know me, from the least of them to the greatest," declares the Lord. "For I will forgive their wickedness and will remember their sins no more." JEREMIAH 31:33–34

Lord our God, we hope in you. One thing never leaves our hearts, your promise that you will be our God, our God in Jesus Christ. This stands firm, and we want to hold to it in trust and confidence. For your Word remains sure, and all your works lead toward a great and wonderful time when you will be glorified, when our hearts can at last become free because we know you. We can become free from all our own works, free from all trembling and hesitation, free from all suffering and distress, because we know that you, O God, are our Father. Amen.

15
September

"For my thoughts are not your thoughts, neither are your ways my ways," declares the Lord. "As the heavens are higher than the earth, so are my ways higher than your ways and my thoughts than your thoughts."

ISAIAH 55:8–9

Lord our God, we thank you for allowing us to come to you and to stand before your face. We thank you for helping us throughout our life on earth, for strengthening our faith in you and our trust in all you do. Bless us and give us courage. May your light shine out among the peoples so that they recognize your will. May your light shine out so that your name may be praised and we can rejoice in the new time you give us. For you will be at work and you will accomplish it. Even when we do not know what will become of our time, you know what our time needs, and you will carry out your will. You will let your name be honored. You will bring your kingdom, and you will change everything for the good. Amen.

16

September

When the Advocate comes, whom I will send to you from the Father – the Spirit of truth who goes out from the Father – he will testify about me. And you also must testify, for you have been with me from the beginning.

JOHN 15:26–27

Great God and Savior, you want to lead us by the hand so that in communion with you we learn how to live a true life. We thank you for everything we have already received. Guide us still, we pray. Through your Spirit lead us in all areas of our life. Grant us the Spirit, who can illumine our hearts to help us find new courage and new strength and new recognition of the truth. All our praise belongs to you, for you alone can quicken us. You alone free us from the pain of death and from all burdens, so that in spite of toil and struggle we may always be lifted up to you, our God on high, to the glory of your name on earth. Amen.

17

September

People were overwhelmed with amazement. "He has done everything well," they said. "He even makes the deaf hear and the mute speak." MARK 7:37

Lord our God, you fill heaven and earth with your Spirit and allow us to share in your gifts. We thank you for all you have given us, for all you are giving and will give. We are poor and needy in spite of our striving, longing, and seeking. Only you, through your Spirit, can awaken something in us to help us go toward your goal. Keep us from being caught up in what people do. The greatest help for our hearts is what you do. Each of us has received help beyond anything we had hoped or thought of. How much you have done for us! How much you are doing for the nations! Yes, we thank you for this present time. Although our lives often seem hopeless and full of sorrow, your powers are still living among us, working for our good and awaking us to new life. The time will surely come when our hearts will be released from their hunger and we can be filled with the life from above, which you give us in Jesus Christ. Amen.

18

September

The twelve gates were twelve pearls, each gate made of a single pearl. The great street of the city was of gold, as pure as transparent glass. I did not see a temple in the city, because the Lord God Almighty and the Lamb are its temple. The city does not need the sun or the moon to shine on it, for the glory of God gives it light, and the Lamb is its lamp. REVELATION 21:21–23

Lord our God, we thank you that you have given us your glorious future as the basis for our lives. We thank you that on this foundation we can forget our present troubles and believe that the power of good can move us today to oppose sin, death, and everything evil. Free our hearts from all burdens, and grant that we may have courage to wait patiently for the great help which is to come. Grant that what is happening in the world today may somehow help toward the solution of all the problems. We praise your name, our Father in the heavens. We praise you for the good you do for us each day and for the light you will shed one day on everything on earth, to the glory of your name. Amen.

19
September

You yourselves have seen what I did to Egypt, and how I carried you on eagles' wings and brought you to myself. Now if you obey me fully and keep my covenant, then out of all nations you will be my treasured possession. Although the whole earth is mine, you will be for me a kingdom of priests and a holy nation. EXODUS 19:4–6A

Lord our God and our Father, we thank you for all the light you let shine on earth to gladden our hearts. Your light shows us how to live in your creation with open eyes and open hearts, accepting in a childlike way all the good gifts from your hand. How much good you send to many sorrowful hearts, and how much strengthening to those in weakness, poverty, and sickness! Grant that we may recognize what comes from you, that we are not cast down in spirit but mount up again and again on wings like eagles. May we learn to say at all times, "Through how much need has not our merciful God spread out his wings to protect us!" Amen.

20

September

Great is the Lord and most worthy of praise; his greatness no one can fathom. One generation commends your works to another; they tell of your mighty acts. They speak of the glorious splendor of your majesty – and I will meditate on your wonderful works. PSALM 145:3–5

Lord God, our Helper, we thank you for walking among us and for letting many experience your protection. Even when we are dying, you protect and help us so that we need not pass into death but may enter into life. So may our hearts be lifted up to you. Grant that the light in us remains undimmed, and that we may come before you in sincerity. Lord God, create good out of evil. Let light dawn in the darkness. Fulfill your promise, for our hearts are not concerned with human desires but with your promise. You will carry it out, and we will be able to say, "Our faith was not in vain, our hope was not in vain. Lord our God, you have blest us a thousandfold." Amen.

21

September

On the last and greatest day of the festival, Jesus stood and said in a loud voice, "Let anyone who is thirsty come to me and drink. Whoever believes in me, as Scripture has said, rivers of living water will flow from within them." JOHN 7:37–38

Dear Father in heaven, we thank you for sending down powers from on high into our earthly life. We thank you for sending us a higher nature in which we can live for others because we are living by what we receive from you. May we be simple, childlike, and trusting. When anyone despairs of himself, show him the way to the Savior so that he can find trust. Show to us the way of trust, trust for ourselves and for all people, because it is your will for all to receive help. Amen.

22
September

He does not treat us as our sins deserve or repay us according to our iniquities. For as high as the heavens are above the earth, so great is his love for those who fear him; as far as the east is from the west, so far has he removed our transgressions from us. PSALM 103:10–12

Lord our God, we lift our hearts to you, for you have given great promises to those who fear you. Let your Word strengthen us in faith, patience, and hope. Be with all those who call upon you, pleading for help in our time. For these times must work for our good, and in spite of sin, death, and all evil we can find joy in what you are doing. We call to you, O Lord our God. Let your hand be revealed, that something may be seen besides human striving and the efforts of human hands. Let the work of your hand be visible to many, to all peoples on this earth. May your name be honored, O Lord our God, your kingdom come, and your will be done on earth as in heaven. Amen.

23

September

This is why it says: "When he ascended on high, he took many captives and gave gifts to his people."

EPHESIANS 4:8

Our dear Father in heaven, we thank you that you have given us the Lord Jesus on high and that we are allowed to be with him and find joy even while still surrounded by all that must fade and perish. For in Jesus Christ you hold us by the hand through anxiety, need, and death. Grant that he may be with us as we continue our pilgrimage. Grant us your Spirit, for we are poor in spirit and in soul. Give us your Holy Spirit from on high. Just in our weakness we come to know what strength and victory you bring through the Lord Jesus, our Savior. The Lord Jesus is our Savior for body, soul, and spirit for ever and ever. Amen.

24
September

Very truly I tell you, unless a kernel of wheat falls to the ground and dies, it remains only a single seed. But if it dies, it produces many seeds. Anyone who loves their life will lose it, while anyone who hates their life in this world will keep it for eternal life. JOHN 12:24–25

Dear Father in heaven, we long to be your children and to grow closer and closer to eternal life with all its goodness and truth. In your love to us your children, bless us as we walk on earth under great stress and temptation. Keep us from going astray, and let what you have placed in our hearts grow toward perfection, to your glory and your honor. May our hearts always know the joy that our struggle and suffering are not in vain, that if we are faithful, we may bring forth the fruit of righteousness. Amen.

25
September

Then I saw a new heaven and a new earth, for the first heaven and the first earth had passed away, and there was no longer any sea...He who was seated on the throne said, "I am making everything new!" Then he said, "Write this down, for these words are trustworthy and true." REVELATION 21:1, 5

Lord our God, our Father, we look deep into your mighty Word and see the glory of the new world you will create according to your justice and truth. We thank you for giving us this joy on earth in the midst of all our toil and striving. We look deep into your Word. You make all things new. To this hope our lives are directed, to this hope you have called us, and we want to be faithful forever. Praise to your name, for you have already done great things for us! Keep us in your Word. Let many find the light, for in this light they may look to you in simple faith and constancy until the end, when throughout the world we may see your glory and your grace. Amen.

26

September

Here I am! I stand at the door and knock. If anyone hears my voice and opens the door, I will come in and eat with that person, and they with me. REVELATION 3:20

Lord our God, we are your children, who come before you and stand in your presence. Be with us and be our light in all situations of life, in all hardships and grief. Be our light, as you have always been. Reveal your power so that the world may know you as we have come to know you. Give us joyful readiness to persevere until your day comes, for the brightness of your day will shine through all darkness and will end all evil, to the glory of your name. Amen.

27

September

I will praise you, Lord, with all my heart; before the "gods" I will sing your praise. I will bow down toward your holy temple and will praise your name for your unfailing love and your faithfulness, for you have so exalted your solemn decree that it surpasses your fame.

PSALM 138:1–2

Dear Father in heaven, we thank you for your mercy and for your great goodness and power, revealed to us through the ages and in the present time. We live by your revelation, Lord God Almighty, for you perform wonders on earth and you reign in heaven so that heaven can bless and help us on our earthly pilgrimage. Grant that your loving-kindness and your justice may be revealed through all the world. Come, O Lord our God, bring the light for us who believe in you, and be the light for the whole world. Glory to your name, for you are indeed our Father in heaven and on earth, and you give certainty for our life in time and in eternity. Amen.

28

September

Give thanks to the Lord, for he is good; his love endures forever. Let the redeemed of the Lord tell their story – those he redeemed from the hand of the foe, those he gathered from the lands, from east and west, from north and south. PSALM 107:1–3

Lord our God and our Father, we thank you for all the blessings you have brought into our lives and for everything we still hope to receive from your goodness. We thank you that through your Spirit you will work more and more in us and in all people, so that we are not held back by any human considerations but can go toward a higher goal. Keep us in your care. In all our special concerns may each of us experience your comfort and help, so that we may rejoice with the praise of your name always in our hearts. Amen.

29
September

A woman giving birth to a child has pain because her time has come; but when her baby is born she forgets the anguish because of her joy that a child is born into the world. So with you: Now is your time of grief, but I will see you again and you will rejoice, and no one will take away your joy. JOHN 16:21–22

Dear Father in heaven, grant us your Spirit so that here on earth we may be united with you in Jesus Christ the Savior. May truth dawn on us with its light, bringing joy no matter what happens to us. May all the pain in our lives be turned into birth pangs of a new life in which we can rejoice as people you have created, people prepared for the struggle on earth, who are called into battle and led to victory. Grant that we may not be blinded by the surrounding darkness. Shed a clear light on the new life that is coming. May we see what has already happened because Jesus Christ came to the earth and remains on earth, and may we see what is still to come through him, the Savior. O God of wonders, keep us aware of the wonders that increasingly surround us, until all the pain on earth is finally overcome. Amen.

30

September

I have told you these things, so that in me you may have peace. In this world you will have trouble. But take heart! I have overcome the world. JOHN 16:33

Dear Father in heaven, in the world we are full of fear; in you we have peace. We pray that your Spirit may give us the joy of your heavenly kingdom and the strength to live in your service. Remember those who suffer pain, who still have to walk paths of fear and distress. Grant them help, to the glory of your name. May we be united in hope and in expectation of what you will give through your great goodness and faithfulness. Amen.

October

1

October

Be joyful in hope, patient in affliction, faithful in prayer… Rejoice with those who rejoice; mourn with those who mourn. ROMANS 12:12, 15

Lord our God, we thank you for your gospel, the great, good tidings we may carry in our hearts to give us joy in this present time, even though on all sides people are in anguish and agony. We thank you that your gospel fills our hearts with compassion, enabling us to help carry what many have to suffer. Show us our need of you so that we can receive your help. If we must be the first to suffer all kinds of pain and distress, may we do so joyfully because we have been promised blessing in the midst of all the pain. May we continually honor your name, praising you for the good news of your kingdom, for the promise that everything must work together for good through Jesus Christ the Savior. Amen.

2

October

In you, Lord, I have taken refuge; let me never be put to shame; deliver me in your righteousness. Turn your ear to me, come quickly to my rescue; be my rock of refuge, a strong fortress to save me. PSALM 31:1–2

Lord our God, give us your Spirit, we beseech you, that we may find your paths on earth and live in the hope and certainty that everything is in your hands, even when we see much that is unjust and evil. May we remain under your protection, living by your commandments and in your Spirit. For your Spirit witnesses to the truth and longs to change and lift up our lives. Your Spirit longs to reach all people who have felt your touch, longs that they may come to you and have life. Amen.

3

October

All this is from God, who reconciled us to himself through Christ and gave us the ministry of reconciliation: that God was reconciling the world to himself in Christ, not counting people's sins against them. And he has committed to us the message of reconciliation.

2 CORINTHIANS 5:18–19

Lord our God, our Father in heaven, we come to you as your children. Bless us, we pray. Bless us especially in days when fear tries to take hold of us. Let your help come down to us as you have promised, the great help in Jesus Christ, who shall come to redeem the whole world. Bless us through your Word. Renew us again and again to stand firm and true to you, for you are our help for redemption and reconciliation through Jesus Christ. Amen.

4

October

He looked up to heaven and with a deep sigh said to him, "Ephphatha!" (which means "Be opened!"). At this, the man's ears were opened, his tongue was loosened and he began to speak plainly. MARK 7:34–35

Father in heaven, we people on earth are poor and needy. We are deaf and dumb, but you rouse us every day and call to us, "Ephphatha." We thank you for this, in gladness for all you do for our sake. Help us to become united in expectation for the great day when our Lord Jesus Christ will come, when before all people he will be proved your Son, the Savior in whom you, the Almighty, come to meet us. Through him you say again, "Let there be light! Let there be life! Let life break free from the darkness of death so that Jesus may come as the Savior of all, the Savior even of those who are still in deepest darkness." Praise to your name, O Father in heaven. Amen.

5
October

He says: "It is too small a thing for you to be my servant to restore the tribes of Jacob and bring back those of Israel I have kept. I will also make you a light for the Gentiles, that my salvation may reach to the ends of the earth."

ISAIAH 49:6

Mighty God, we thank you for sending your light into all the world to reveal that you are the Father of all, to show us that you are leading them to yourself, the good and the bad, those who are near to you and those who are far away. We thank you that through all this your name may be acknowledged and honored. We thank you that we may live from your hand and that everyone may see your work on earth and be filled with praise. May the light which you have sent to earth in Jesus Christ shine brightly for us and penetrate our hearts so that we open ourselves to it with joy, and worship the Savior. Bless us and give us your Spirit; without your Spirit we can do nothing. May we receive help from you every day. Amen.

6

October

Righteous Father, though the world does not know you, I know you, and they know that you have sent me. I have made you known to them, and will continue to make you known in order that the love you have for me may be in them and that I myself may be in them. JOHN 17:25–26

Lord our God, our Father, give us your Spirit, we pray, for you have ruled over us at all times and loved us with a love that guides and leads us, that helps us go forward in body and soul. Reveal your hand. Grant that we undertake nothing in human strength; may everything come from you for each one whose heart holds true to you and who does the work intended for him. Then everything we do on earth can be a service to you. Protect us through your great goodness and faithfulness, which have been with us to this day and will go with us into the future. Amen.

7
October

I am the good shepherd; I know my sheep and my sheep know me – just as the Father knows me and I know the Father – and I lay down my life for the sheep.

JOHN 10:14–15

Dear Father in heaven, we thank you that your voice reaches our hearts and that we can say with joy, "We belong to you. We too are yours." We want to lead lives that show we belong to you, never allowing ourselves to be sidetracked, never again giving way to pettiness, always drawing strength from the power of Jesus Christ. Protect our household. Watch over each of us. Protect us all on our way. O mighty God, be with us in the many dangers that surround us, and grant that we may always be joyful because our names are recorded in heaven. Amen.

8

October

Therefore, dear friends, since you have been forewarned, be on your guard so that you may not be carried away by the error of the lawless and fall from your secure position. But grow in the grace and knowledge of our Lord and Savior Jesus Christ. To him be glory both now and forever! Amen. 2 PETER 3:17–18

Lord our God, we thank you for giving us a strong fortress in Jesus, the only Lord, with whom we can oppose the whole raging, hateful, lawless, and cruel world. Come what may, we want to hold high the banner of Jesus Christ. In him we want to wait for the time when your mighty deeds will fully establish your kingdom for all nations on earth. You are our God and our Father. Protect us, and give light to our hearts so that we can always be joyful and can hope in you forevermore. Amen.

9
October

Great and marvelous are your deeds, Lord God Almighty. Just and true are your ways, King of the nations. Who will not fear you, Lord, and bring glory to your name? For you alone are holy. All nations will come and worship before you, for your righteous acts have been revealed. REVELATION 15:3–4

O Lord God, we thank you that in our times we may feel and see that you are at work. This is a joy and comfort to us and we take heart, although the misery on earth sometimes brings us to tears. We find joy again because you are at work. You are carrying out your will, which includes your plan for our life and salvation. Grant that fruits may appear in our times, for our times are in your hands. Grant that many people from all nations may come to you. May they turn to you in their need and know the happiness of receiving your help. May your name be honored, your kingdom come, and your will be done on earth as in heaven. Amen.

10
October

For all have sinned and fall short of the glory of God, and all are justified freely by his grace through the redemption that came by Christ Jesus. God presented Christ as a sacrifice of atonement, through the shedding of his blood – to be received by faith. ROMANS 3:23–25A

Lord our God, we praise your name because you have set up a mercy seat on earth, because you forgive our sins through the blood of Jesus Christ. May your mercy be seen at work in many hearts. Shed your light upon all people, and let your glory be known. Let your glory shine in all hearts, to the praise of your name and the deliverance of those who are still in misery. Keep us in your Word, which works miracles. Protect in us all that Jesus Christ has brought to the earth, and may we use his gifts in simplicity of heart. Grant that much may be accomplished to the glory of your name and that we may draw nearer to the day of Jesus Christ, for which we wait in hope and longing. Amen.

11

October

Trust in the Lord and do good; dwell in the land and enjoy safe pasture. Take delight in the Lord, and he will give you the desires of your heart. PSALM 37:3–4

Dear Father in heaven, we love and honor your ways even when they are bitter ways. We long for courage and strength. Lord, help us to believe. Grant faith to the millions surrounded by death, faith that overcomes everything through utmost self-denial. Let your light shine out to bring life to the nations in the midst of all that is happening. Your light shall lead and guide us, and peace will come, a deeper peace than we have ever known. Remember each of us in all our concerns, and grant that the struggles of life may lead us to peace. If hard and bitter ways should be our lot, help us to remain steadfast, never complaining about our burdens even in the most difficult days, for through grief and trouble the way leads to you. Amen.

12
October

And forgive us our debts, as we also have forgiven our debtors. MATTHEW 6:12

Lord our God, we thank you for the great light you send throughout the world to let us know that you forgive, that no sin is too great for you to forgive. Grant that people may cry out, "Have mercy on me, O God!" Give them the spirit of prayer in their hearts to call, "Father, forgive us our sins." Send your Holy Spirit, the Spirit of truth and humility, and then forgive their sins. Wherever a soul is sighing, wherever someone is calling to you, hear him. May our prayers come before your throne. Hear and answer us. We have so much on our hearts that we cannot rightly express it all. We pray for others too. Father, forgive them. Clear away all the obstacles so that your judgment can be merciful toward those whom you forgive. Be with us. May we be a church community of Jesus Christ, washed in his blood, with strength to face every bitter outburst of the world's fury and still forgive. May our prayer remain, "Forgive us our sins as we forgive those who sin against us." Amen.

13
October

Because you are his sons, God sent the Spirit of his Son into our hearts, the Spirit who calls out, "Abba, Father." So you are no longer a slave, but God's child; and since you are his child, God has made you also an heir.

GALATIANS 4:6–7

Dear Father in heaven, we come before you as your children, longing to be assured through your Spirit that we are and may remain your children. We long to live to the glory of your name under the shelter and guidance of the Lord Jesus in expectation of the great day which shall fulfill all promises made to us. Strengthen us, especially in dark and troubled days. Help us when danger threatens and when evil tries to make headway among us. Deliver us from all evil, for yours is the kingdom, the power, and the glory for ever and ever. Amen.

14
October

I will listen to what God the Lord says; he promises peace to his people, his faithful servants – but let them not turn to folly. Surely his salvation is near those who fear him, that his glory may dwell in our land. PSALM 85:8–9

Lord our God, you are help, comfort, and life to us in everything we have to endure. We gather before you as poor, weak people, but you can make us rich and give us new life so that our lives prove we hold to your will and to the justice you bring on earth. May we be one in spirit through all we experience in our hearts, to the glory of your name. May the praise and thanks of many people ring out into all the world because you are help and deliverance from all evil. Amen.

15

October

On hearing this, Jesus said, "It is not the healthy who need a doctor, but the sick. But go and learn what this means: 'I desire mercy, not sacrifice.' For I have not come to call the righteous, but sinners." MATTHEW 9:12–13

Dear Father in heaven, we come into your presence as imperfect, sinful children, who do many foolish things and who are involved in much that is evil and corrupt. We come to you, Father, knowing that your fatherly love is with us through all eternity. Be gracious to us and free us from all the harm and injury we are bound to suffer in this earthly life. May the grace your kingdom brings on earth finally blot out the sins of all people, so that as your children they may rejoice because you have helped them. May your name be praised among all people. Amen.

16
October

I always thank my God for you because of his grace given you in Christ Jesus. For in him you have been enriched in every way – with all kinds of speech and with all knowledge. 1 CORINTHIANS 1:4–5

Lord our God, we thank you that you are so near to us that we may feel and know we are your children, your children who are in your hands with all that belongs to our earthly life, all our needs and temptations, all our efforts and pain. We come together to thank you, and our thanksgiving wins a victory over everything that makes life difficult for us. In this thanksgiving the harshness, crookedness, and injustice on earth cannot harm us. Protect us with your light, which gives us wisdom for all situations and which lifts us above everything that is base and meaningless and must pass away. Amen.

17
October

The night is nearly over; the day is almost here. So let us put aside the deeds of darkness and put on the armor of light. ROMANS 13:12

Father in heaven, we thank you for giving us light. We thank you for the great hope for a day whose light is not of our making, whose source is in you, a day to come that can touch our lives already today. Keep our hearts steadfast, free of all human wavering. May we always hold to the love you have given through your grace, and may we find joy in your love, which is full of light and understanding. Amen.

18

October

Jesus replied: "'Love the Lord your God with all your heart and with all your soul and with all your mind.' This is the first and greatest commandment. And the second is like it: 'Love your neighbor as yourself.'"

MATTHEW 22:37–39

Lord our God, through your Spirit help us to live in love to you. Open our eyes to see your goodness and truth surrounding us your children, even in this troubled world. We look to you, Almighty Father. Protect us in these difficult times. We plead for our country, entrusting it to your care so that love to you may be awakened. Where shall we turn except to you? Where shall we find help except in Jesus Christ, whom you have sent to us to win the victory, to subdue and end all evil in heaven, on earth, and under the earth, and to become Lord, to the glory of your name? Amen.

19

October

And the peace of God, which transcends all understanding, will guard your hearts and your minds in Christ Jesus. PHILIPPIANS 4:7

O Lord God, grant us your Spirit, that we may comprehend your peace. As we pray, help us to recognize what must come from you alone, for you are mighty and holy and your will is peace on earth. Your will is peace beyond all understanding, your peace in heaven and on earth and under the earth, your peace that opposes all sin and death and takes away every evil that can be named. We await you, O Lord our God, and you will hear us. No matter how long the battle lasts, we hold out in patience, for we are your children. We shall never lose the faith that your name shall be honored and that all things shall come into harmony with your will of peace on earth, your peace. Amen.

20
October

Let all the earth fear the Lord; let all the people of the world revere him. For he spoke, and it came to be; he commanded, and it stood firm. The Lord foils the plans of the nations; he thwarts the purposes of the peoples.

PSALM 33:8–10

Lord our God, we gather together in your presence and ask you to let your light shine in our hearts to strengthen us in times of need and trouble. May we come to know that through all the storms and distress of the world, you are mighty in protecting and sheltering those who trust in you. May we realize the power of your kingdom. Even if all the kingdoms of the world rise in rebellion, you are with us. You are with those who have set their hope on your kingdom and who go on hoping that even in evil days something must happen through your great and holy rule. Amen.

21

October

Another angel, who had a golden censer, came and stood at the altar. He was given much incense to offer, with the prayers of all God's people, on the golden altar in front of the throne. The smoke of the incense, together with the prayers of God's people, went up before God from the angel's hand. REVELATION 8:3–4

Lord God, we come before you and ask you to turn our hearts and minds to you alone, to you who have power over the whole world and who can do everything in our hearts according to your will. Let there be light in our time. Hear and answer the many prayers that have already come to you, rising for centuries before your throne, prayers for your kingdom and for your will on earth. This earth has become the prey of evil. We are poor and needy, and you alone can help us. Help us, O Lord, our God and Father. After this misery let your day come, your great day over all the world and over all peoples. Amen.

22

October

And now, Israel, what does the Lord your God ask of you but to fear the Lord your God, to walk in obedience to him, to love him, to serve the Lord your God with all your heart and with all your soul? DEUTERONOMY 10:12

Lord our God, our Father in heaven, be with us as we are gathered here. Through your Spirit let our hearts grow in understanding of how we can serve you rightly and live as you want us to live. Help us hold fast to all that is good. Free us more and more from everything that hinders us, from all that is evil. Show your loving-kindness to us and to our loved ones, wherever they may be. Hear every human heart that sighs to you, pleading that what is of heaven may overcome what is of earth. Amen.

23
October

Praise be to the God and Father of our Lord Jesus Christ, the Father of compassion and the God of all comfort, who comforts us in all our troubles, so that we can comfort those in any trouble with the comfort we ourselves receive from God. For just as we share abundantly in the sufferings of Christ, so also our comfort abounds through Christ. 2 CORINTHIANS 1:3–5

Lord our God, Father of compassion and the God of all comfort, who encourages and strengthens us in all distress, we thank you for turning our suffering into a pathway to life, so that we may be thankful and trusting through everything. You can change what we find hardest into what is best for us. Praise to your name that a way through sin and death is given to us. Praise to your name that you have shown us a way through all evil, a way that is blest. Amen.

24
October

No, the Father himself loves you because you have loved me and have believed that I came from God. JOHN 16:27

Dear Father in heaven, we thank you that with our poor, faulty, sinful, and death-ridden lives we may find shelter in your love. We thank you that we are your children. We thank you that whatever we are, however depressed we are about ourselves and the inadequacy of our own nature, we are still your children. Give us your Spirit, we pray. Give us your Holy Spirit, penetrating our whole nature, our flesh and blood, keeping us firm in faith under all temptation and distress. Give us your Spirit to fill us with hope as we look to the future, to fill us with certainty in our Lord Jesus Christ, who was, and is, and is to come, whose victory is before our eyes so that we never waver or become afraid. Give us your Spirit so that we may live in this certainty and prepare ourselves more and more for your coming into the world. May we come to know that your loving-kindness is at work today, that in the end your deliverance will come quickly, to the glory of your name. Amen.

25
October

When Jesus spoke again to the people, he said, "I am the light of the world. Whoever follows me will never walk in darkness, but will have the light of life." JOHN 8:12

Lord our God, grant that our spirit may recognize your Spirit and your love, so that our lives cannot be swallowed up by passing concerns but are lifted to something higher. Help us hold fast to all the blessings you have allowed us to experience, the blessings you will certainly continue to give, even though new battles and new troubles are all around us. Send a great light to shine among the many people whose task is to lead the way so that your kingdom may come. Send light so that your name may be honored through our human deeds and you may be known as life for all. Amen.

26

October

I will remain in the world no longer, but they are still in the world, and I am coming to you. Holy Father, protect them by the power of your name, the name you gave me, so that they may be one as we are one. JOHN 17:11

Lord Jesus Christ, our Savior, stand at our side and protect us in all our days on earth. Grant us an understanding of the honor that belongs to God. Help us see that you are sent so that heaven and earth shall one day bow down before God's almighty will. Stand by us so that we may hear, understand, and accept your Word. Stand by us all our lives. Be with us in suffering and in our last hour when death comes to us. May your grace be with us. Help us at all times to be firmly rooted in the will of our God and Father in heaven. Amen.

27
October

We are hard pressed on every side, but not crushed; perplexed, but not in despair; persecuted, but not abandoned; struck down, but not destroyed. We always carry around in our body the death of Jesus, so that the life of Jesus may also be revealed in our body.

2 CORINTHIANS 4:8–10

Lord God, we thank you for your voice even when it is stern and we must go through hardship and suffering. Your voice speaks to us, and in your voice we can be glad and victorious in our life on earth. Come into our lives. May each of us realize that all we have gone through has been for the good. Be God and Lord over the nations. Be a refuge for all people . Grant that the sin and distress of this terrible time may soon pass and that we may hear your words, "Be comforted. I will come soon. All these terrors must pass by. My will is being done. My name must be honored. My kingdom and my rule are coming. So take heart and at all times look to your God and Father in heaven." Amen.

28

October

Sacrifice thank offerings to God, fulfill your vows to the Most High, and call on me in the day of trouble; I will deliver you, and you will honor me. PSALM 50:14–15

Dear Father in heaven, we want to praise you together and to thank you with all our hearts for your goodness and your deliverance from our many needs. Accept our thanks, and help us go on our way with ever joyful hearts. Make us ready for whatever you have prepared for us, your children. Bless us in our individual lives and bless us in our community. Let your Spirit shed its rays into all places to comfort people's hearts and to restore and strengthen their faith. May your name be praised forevermore. Amen.

29
October

Blessed are those who have learned to acclaim you, who walk in the light of your presence, Lord. They rejoice in your name all day long; they celebrate your righteousness.

PSALM 89:15–16

Dear Father in heaven, how lovingly you have thought of us! How much good you let us experience again and again! So our hearts are happy, and we go to rest this night full of joy and thanks because we are your children. Our thanks and joy shall be our service to you day and night. More than this you do not ask, and in this we will be faithful. We want to be joyful and to be glad for our lives. Even when we face dark hours, O Lord our God, we are filled with hope that brings us joy for the future as well as for the present, with assurance that your salvation is coming. We rejoice in what you give us already today. Amen.

30
October

Praise the Lord, all you nations; extol him, all you peoples. For great is his love toward us, and the faithfulness of the Lord endures forever. Praise the Lord.

PSALM 117

Lord our God, we thank you that we may come to you and that our spirits can reach out for your help and your comfort. May we draw strength from communion with you, our Father. May we realize more fully that we are your children, truly your children, who throughout our pilgrimage are allowed to know you as our refuge and our help. Remember our world, and grant that many hearts awaken and turn to you, looking to you in all the fear and need which sweep over many people in our time. Let your Spirit be revealed to our hearts in quiet, bringing many experiences from you, O Lord our God, and from your kingdom. Protect us every day in the many lands throughout the earth. For the nations are yours; they shall receive life and blessing from you, and at last your kingdom will be revealed in all the world, to the eternal glory of your name. Amen.

31

October

Let those who fear the Lord say: "His love endures forever." When hard pressed, I cried to the Lord; he brought me into a spacious place. The Lord is with me; I will not be afraid. What can mere mortals do to me?

PSALM 118:4–6

Lord our God, dear Father in heaven, we thank you. How often you rescue us from all fear and distress! How often you hear and answer us! Grant that our hearts may always be eager and joyful because you answer us. There is nothing else for us in this world; you are our one hope, our only hope. You alone can help our times, help the nations, help each person. Nothing else matters to us. Lord our God, for the rest of our life on earth you alone are our help, our comfort, and our strength. Amen.

November

1

November

Let the message of Christ dwell among you richly as you teach and admonish one another with all wisdom through psalms, hymns, and songs from the Spirit, singing to God with gratitude in your hearts. COLOSSIANS 3:16

Dear Father in heaven, we seek you and your kingdom. We gather to hear your Word so that we may receive strength for our own lives and for all our relationships with others. We want to stand firm, believing that in everything great and small your will is being done and that we may yet experience a new coming of your glory on earth. Then earthly concerns will no longer torment us and wear us out, but heavenly things may surround us and everything become new in accordance with your good, merciful, and perfect will. Amen.

2

November

Since, then, you have been raised with Christ, set your hearts on things above, where Christ is, seated at the right hand of God. Set your minds on things above, not on earthly things. COLOSSIANS 3:1–2

Lord our God, we thank you for sending into our lives so much that turns our thoughts to things above and enables us always to look to you. Through Jesus Christ send us what is of heaven. Send what is of heaven into every single life and into the lives of the nations, so that something good may arise and the glory does not go to the Devil but to your Spirit, your heavenly Spirit alone. In their stubbornness people intend to do evil, but you can turn it all to the good. You can change everything. This is our faith. We hope in you, and we want to put our lives in your hands. Bless us with heavenly riches and power. Amen.

3

November

This is the message we have heard from him and declare to you: God is light; in him there is no darkness at all.

1 JOHN 1:5

Lord our God, rule over us in strength, and grant us your light. Let your Spirit be with us to confirm what has already taken place in our hearts, so that we have joy and trust even under all the strain and stress of this life. Shine into the darkness of the world. Shine for all people. May we be shown more and more clearly what we have been created for. Strengthen our faith for the future, our faith in everything good, for however hidden the good may be, it must at last come to the light. May we and all the world bring praise and honor to you. Amen.

4 November

But you have come to Mount Zion, to the city of the living God, the heavenly Jerusalem. You have come to thousands upon thousands of angels in joyful assembly, to the church of the firstborn, whose names are written in heaven. You have come to God, the Judge of all, to the spirits of the righteous made perfect, to Jesus the mediator of a new covenant. HEBREWS 12:22–24A

Lord our God, we thank you that you have redeemed us and that we may feel united with your holy ones, those in heaven and those on earth who are gathered around Jesus Christ, a people growing in number and strength from year to year. We thank you that we too belong to them, and we ask you to keep our hearts aware of this unity so that we may be joyful, redeemed people who find ever greater deliverance, full of praise and thanks, full of certainty and joy. Grant this to us, for we are your people, born out of your power as Savior and gathered for the sake of your kingdom. Guard your gifts and powers within us. Continue your redemption of the whole world until joy floods through our whole being. Amen.

5
November

The eyes of the Lord are on those who love him, a mighty shield and strong support, a shelter from scorching wind and a shade from noonday sun, a guard against stumbling and a help against falling.

ECCLESIASTICUS 34:19, NRSV

Lord God Almighty, whose eyes keep watch over the whole world, we come before you with the evil from our surroundings still clinging to us. Grant that our lives may be in your hands. Give us your strength to find the way, even through suffering and distress. For we are yours, O Lord our God, and you have chosen your people to be strong and to be freed from all evils. Help us, we beseech you. May we know that you are with us and may your Word bring us blessing, to the glory of your name forever. Amen.

6

November

On this mountain he will destroy the shroud that enfolds all peoples, the sheet that covers all nations; he will swallow up death forever. The Sovereign Lord will wipe away the tears from all faces; he will remove his people's disgrace from all the earth. The Lord has spoken.

ISAIAH 25:7–8

Lord our God, your kingdom is coming. Your help reaches us. However much we must suffer, we look to you, for you have given us your promise. You have promised that all shall go well with us. You have promised that while still on earth your people may have strength to trust in you and wait for you in patience and joy. So lay your hands upon us, O Lord our God, and let your redeeming strength be revealed in us. You know all our needs. You see into each heart and know how to help, as you have promised. Bless us and help us, and may your name be honored among us. May your kingdom come, and your will be done on earth as in heaven. Amen.

7
November

Consider the generations of old and see: has anyone trusted in the Lord and been disappointed? Or has anyone persevered in the fear of the Lord and been forsaken? Or has anyone called upon him and been neglected? For the Lord is compassionate and merciful; he forgives sins and saves in time of distress. ECCLESIASTICUS 2:10–11, NRSV

Dear Father in heaven, Mighty God in heaven and on earth, quicken us by the Word you have sent and by all you have done for us in your mercy and steadfast love. Keep us eager and joyful even in difficult and troubled days. Grant us unfailing trust in you, to give us firm ground under our feet so that we can always thank and glorify you. For you, O Lord, are our God. You are our Father, and you will never forsake your children in all eternity. Amen.

8

November

Very truly I tell you, whoever hears my word and believes him who sent me has eternal life and will not be judged but has crossed over from death to life. JOHN 5:24

Lord our God, we thank you for giving us Jesus Christ, whose words remain living to this very day. You will make his words continually alive so that in the name of Jesus Christ joyful praises are sung to you, Almighty God and Father in heaven. Remember us all. Remember the particular needs of each one of us. Come to the world through the words of Jesus Christ. May his words come as your strong angels to the hearts of many to comfort and restore, to help and do miracles for those in need. May your name be praised through the great and mighty Word, Jesus Christ! Amen.

9
November

But in keeping with his promise we are looking forward to a new heaven and a new earth, where righteousness dwells. 2 PETER 3:13

Lord our God, dear Father, may we be gathered in your light. Through your Spirit strengthen our hearts to hold fast to you, for you remain our help, our counsel, our comfort throughout our life and in all eternity. Send us Jesus Christ, the Savior of the world, and grant that again and again we may find newness of life through him. Grant that we become attentive to him, who is risen from the dead and who will come again to complete the work he began in his life on earth. We remember your promise, O Lord God, and we remain with you. We have little strength, and through us as we are you can accomplish nothing. You alone can fulfill your promise through Jesus Christ, whom you will send to complete your works at his final coming. Amen.

10
November

"I am the Alpha and the Omega," says the Lord God, "who is, and who was, and who is to come, the Almighty."

REVELATION 1:8

Lord our God, the Alpha and the Omega, the beginning and the end, who was and is and is to come, the Almighty, we thank you for this wonderful message, which is meant for us too, even though our lives often seem empty and sad. But behold, you make all things new for each one of us. Even though we have long tormented ourselves, the light of life will dawn at last and we will be able to rejoice. Continue to protect us and our community. Wake us to new life, for you have called us to believe and to endure to the end. Whatever sorrows and hardships may come, we will remain faithful, O Lord our God. This is our promise to you. We will persevere and say joyfully, "Jesus Christ is coming to make all things new." Amen.

11 November

I am the Lord your God, who brought you out of Egypt, out of the land of slavery. You shall have no other gods before me. You shall not make for yourself an image in the form of anything in heaven above or on the earth beneath or in the waters below. You shall not bow down to them or worship them; for I, the Lord your God, am a jealous God, punishing the children for the sin of the parents to the third and fourth generation of those who hate me, but showing love to a thousand generations of those who love me and keep my commandments.

EXODUS 20:2–6

Lord our God, we come to you, the source of all being. You have said to us, "I am your God. You shall have no other gods besides me. Honor none but me, your God." We thank you for this wonderful message. Help us to recognize you more and more, so that our hearts are full of the goodness and blessing we already have on earth, so that we hear you, the mighty One, say, "Stop, O people. Make peace. No one of you is more important than any other. Remember that I am God of all, in south and north, in west and east, on the oceans and everywhere. I am the one God, and through Jesus Christ I am now your Father." Amen.

12

November

For you know very well that the day of the Lord will come like a thief in the night…But you, brothers and sisters, are not in darkness so that this day should surprise you like a thief. You are all children of the light and children of the day. We do not belong to the night or to the darkness. I THESSALONIANS 5:2,4–5

Lord our God, we hold to you and to your promise. Though much is hidden from us, your voice comes clearly to us proclaiming, "Watch and pray. You are to await the day of Jesus Christ your Lord, and you can rejoice now in the midst of strife, distress, fear, and need." We thank you for your powerful Word. However long the time of waiting may be, your Word remains eternally and will be fulfilled. Your name shall be honored in the proclamation of your Word, your kingdom shall come, and your will shall be done on earth as in heaven. Amen.

13

November

In the time of those kings, the God of heaven will set up a kingdom that will never be destroyed, nor will it be left to another people. It will crush all those kingdoms and bring them to an end, but it will itself endure forever.

DANIEL 2:44

Lord our God, we thank you that you work in us and in our lives and that you show us your compassion, no matter what cross we have to bear. We want to rejoice in you and wait patiently until your purpose is fulfilled and your kingdom arises on earth. Protect each one of us. May our hearts find strength and never-failing joy in Jesus Christ the Savior, always hoping and believing, always looking to you. For you are the almighty God, who will come in Jesus Christ to establish his kingdom among the peoples and at last reveal his truth in its fullness. Then the knowledge of your will shall spread to all peoples, so that good and evil may come before you and be judged according to your mercy and faithful love. Amen.

14
November

"The days are coming," declares the Lord, *"when I will fulfill the good promise I made to the people of Israel and Judah."* JEREMIAH 33:14

Lord our God, may your grace rule in our hearts and your love come to us in glorious fulfillment of your promise, so that in our time we may have community with one another to praise and worship you. Then we will be a people belonging to you and receiving help from you. Bless your Word within us, we pray. Teach us again and again how to keep your Word, how to be your children in deed and in truth. May we be given strength of heart whenever great sorrow comes to us. Let your will be revealed everywhere. Let all of humankind know that you rule, that you help us and will remain with us into all eternity. For our names are recorded with you, and we want to stay with you, Father in heaven. We want nothing else but to be your children in this world, to be children in your care for all eternity. Amen.

15

November

The land yields its harvest; God, our God, blesses us. May God bless us still, so that all the ends of the earth will fear him. PSALM 67:6–7

Lord our God, bless us, that the world may be blest. Help us, that the whole world may be helped. Grant us your mercy in Jesus Christ, who laid down his life for the whole world. May it soon be revealed that your kingdom stands and will bring our age to an end, a good and blessed end. Grant your blessing on every aspect of our lives, on all the concerns and requests we have on our hearts, and help us to praise and thank you every day. Let your will become known everywhere in spite of the horror and blasphemy, so that even the dying may glorify you and all who have to suffer may praise and thank you because they see your face and recognize your light. We want to entrust everything to you, Lord God. We await you. We rejoice and thank you, for we know your will shall be done. We know and believe that your name shall be glorified. Amen.

16
November

Now faith is confidence in what we hope for and assurance about what we do not see. HEBREWS 11:1

Lord our God, we come to you in community of faith and trust, in expectation that you will act. May our hearts be strengthened in all the pain and in all the conflicts of our world. Reveal your will, Almighty God, and protect those you have appointed as our leaders and rulers. Let your will be made plain to them. O Lord God, help your people in these times and give them strength to wait expectantly for what is good, to live and serve in this expectation. Grant your help to all who strive for this. We can all tell of the help that comes from you, for you always support us with your power, also in hard times. Amen.

17
November

What answer shall be given to the envoys of that nation? "The Lord has established Zion, and in her his afflicted people will find refuge." ISAIAH 14:32

Lord our God, you are our refuge. We wait for you, for your purpose will never fail and your promise will be fulfilled. This we may firmly believe, and from this we may draw strength every day. Even when our life brings sorrow, we do not want to grieve. We want to hope and believe and endure until your day comes. Your kingdom will come on earth, and in the meantime you are watching over your people. In the midst of the world's daily affairs there will be people who hope in you, who belong to you, and who are firmly rooted in the grace of Jesus Christ until the time is fulfilled. Amen.

18

November

Rejoice greatly, O daughter of Zion! Shout aloud, O daughter of Jerusalem! Lo, your king comes to you; triumphant and victorious is he, humble and riding on an ass, on a colt the foal of an ass. ZECHARIAH 9:9, RSV

Lord our God, we stand before you and rejoice that you want to be our Helper, our Father. We live in a dark and evil time when whole nations groan and lament. Our need rises to you in heaven, and we cry out, "Help us, Lord our God!" Help that your will may be done in all things and that your kingdom may come. Our task is to pray to you at all times, calling, "Come, O Lord God, in Jesus Christ, the Lord and Savior of all the world!" For in east and west, in south and north, among all nations, Jesus Christ is Lord and Savior. Praise to your name that you have given us this Lord. Amen.

19
November

But God chose the foolish things of the world to shame the wise; God chose the weak things of the world to shame the strong. I CORINTHIANS 1:27

Lord our God, we come to you poor and yet rich, weak and yet strong, with the prayer that your promise may be fulfilled in Jesus Christ, our dear Lord and Savior. Let the time come when the heavens open and a new light shines over the earth, a time when people will praise and thank you and receive everlasting peace and happiness with you. Remember the many people who come into need these days. Remember our nation and all who work for the good of our country. Bless them and help them. And help the dying, O Lord our God; grant that they come to you, for they are yours. Your help will bring life out of death, joy out of grief and need. May your name be honored, dear Father in heaven, may your kingdom come and your will be done on earth as in heaven. Amen.

20

November

Lord, my strength and my fortress, my refuge in time of distress, to you the nations will come from the ends of the earth and say, "Our ancestors possessed nothing but false gods, worthless idols that did them no good."

JEREMIAH 16:19

Lord our God, we come to you burdened and driven by every kind of need and oppression, but you will bring light into every situation; in your great goodness and faithfulness you will continue to help. We come to you because you are our help. We want to draw strength from your Word so that we can remain steadfast in these times, awaiting your help and already finding joy and certainty in our expectation. For your kingdom is coming, and your will is being done on earth as in heaven. Amen.

21

November

Take the helmet of salvation and the sword of the Spirit, which is the word of God. And pray in the Spirit on all occasions with all kinds of prayers and requests. With this in mind, be alert and always keep on praying for all the Lord's people. EPHESIANS 6:17–18

Lord God, whose might is over all the world, over heaven and over earth, we want to find strength in you, for you have given us thousands of proofs that you are with us, helping in all that happens. And when we meet with difficulties, we want all the more to find strength in you, we want all the more to hope in you and await your victory. Let your light shine into everything, in life and in death. For yours is the kingdom, the power, and the glory for ever and ever. Amen.

22

November

Be patient, then, brothers and sisters, until the Lord's coming. See how the farmer waits for the land to yield its valuable crop, patiently waiting for the autumn and spring rains. JAMES 5:7

Lord Jesus, hear our prayer and reveal your hand in our days. May those things be done that bring your future nearer and that let the world see you as the Savior who can lead us to our Father. Bless your Word within us. May our hearts be strengthened, and may we always live in your presence. We draw our life from your Word, from your promise, and we set our hope on you, our Lord and Savior. Show your might, Lord Jesus, and carry out the will of God over all the world, so that we may rejoice when we see God's glory appear and his will being done on earth as in heaven. Amen.

23
November

I am the good shepherd. The good shepherd lays down his life for the sheep. The hired hand is not the shepherd and does not own the sheep. So when he sees the wolf coming, he abandons the sheep and runs away. Then the wolf attacks the flock and scatters it. JOHN 10:11–12

Lord our God, we thank you for ruling us with your shepherd's staff so that again and again we can be refreshed and can delight in what you are doing for us. We thank you that we can have eager, joyful faith even when sorrows come, looking again and again to the good you give us. We are thankful and want to be thankful always. Be a mighty Lord over the peoples, we pray, and protect our country. Show your sovereignty by guarding the flock close beside you and by pouring out your grace to give life to the dying and resurrection to those who have died. O Lord God, hear and bless us. May your will be done on earth as in heaven, so that your kingdom may break in and everything may come right, according to your great purpose. Amen.

24
November

Do not think that I have come to abolish the Law or the Prophets; I have not come to abolish them but to fulfill them…For I tell you that unless your righteousness surpasses that of the Pharisees and the teachers of the law, you will certainly not enter the kingdom of heaven.

MATTHEW 5:17, 20

O Lord God, give us new hearts. Teach us a new way, so that through your commandments all people may act in accordance with your Word and may become one. Only you can do this, working through your promised Holy Spirit, that the earth may become a paradise, a heavenly kingdom pleasing to you. Let your words be written in our hearts, and help us fulfill your commandments in our daily life. Only by carrying out your commandments may we foolish, sinful people be made perfect, our sins be forgiven, and everything become right and good in your sight. Stay with us, Lord God, our Father. Help us in everything. Let something new, pleasing to you, soon come into our time. Put your commandments into our hearts, that peace may be restored to the glory of your name. Amen.

25
November

The Lord reigns, let the earth be glad; let the distant shores rejoice…The heavens proclaim his righteousness, and all peoples see his glory. PSALM 97:1, 6

Lord our God, we turn to you, for you are our help. Hear our prayer, we beseech you; let our cry rise to you so that you may send your mighty help in our generation. Continue to protect us from all evil, from death and destruction. Protect us because we are your children. As your children we turn to you, the almighty God, who can make everything work together for good. Be merciful to us, O Lord God. Help us for your name's sake. Help, Lord, for you alone can bring everything to a good end. So we stand before you in Jesus Christ, holding to every word you have given us and knowing for certain that you hear us. Amen.

26

November

Oh, that you would rend the heavens and come down, that the mountains would tremble before you! As when fire sets twigs ablaze and causes water to boil, come down to make your name known to your enemies and cause the nations to quake before you! ISAIAH 64:1–2

Lord our God, in our times too you hear the prayers and cries of your children. We need to cry out, for humankind has not become your own but still lives in pain and under judgment, and many thousands have to die or undergo terrible things. They should be yours, every one of them. They should all be your children. So we cry out to you: Reveal and glorify your name on earth so that a new time may come and great wonders may be done by your hand. May your name be honored, your kingdom come, and your will be done on earth as in heaven. Amen.

27
November

Good and upright is the Lord; therefore he instructs sinners in his ways. He guides the humble in what is right and teaches them his way. PSALM 25:8–9

Lord our God, dear Father in heaven, we thank you that we may be your children, led by you. We thank you for guiding us in times of grief and never forsaking us. Now, as of old, you are with us, Lord our God, and you show us the way in every situation. Protect us in this present time, and grant us strength to go on patiently even when our lives hold much suffering and distress. We thank you for your guidance and rejoice in your help for our time. Reveal your hand in power, for soon, very soon, your right hand will change everything. Amen.

28
November

Be on guard! Be alert! You do not know when that time will come. It's like a man going away: He leaves his house and puts his servants in charge, each with their assigned task, and tells the one at the door to keep watch. Therefore keep watch because you do not know when the owner of the house will come back – whether in the evening, or at midnight, or when the rooster crows, or at dawn. If he comes suddenly, do not let him find you sleeping. What I say to you, I say to everyone: "Watch!" MARK 13:33–37

Lord Jesus, our Savior, we look upward to heaven, for you will come from heaven in the glory of the Father. May we remain true to our calling, watching and praying every day and every hour, waiting for you, who will bring into order everything on earth. Bless us and bless our land. Grant us the joy to see you working through your servants toward the salvation of the peoples. Be with us and bless us. May your living Word work in our hearts so that every Sunday, every festival, and every day from now on may be a day of joy. Protect us. Bless us. May your name be praised in our hearts! Amen.

29
November

Very truly I tell you, whoever believes in me will do the works I have been doing, and they will do even greater things than these, because I am going to the Father.

JOHN 14:12

Lord our God, we call to you, "Abba, dear Father!" because your Spirit draws us to Jesus Christ the Savior and to his gospel. We call to you for we belong to your kingdom. Give us strength to remain steadfast through all the troubles of our lives. Let your hand remain over us and over the warring nations. Your hand directs, your hand carries out the thoughts of your heart. May the time soon come when you will bring everything to fulfillment and give peace on earth. In expectation we praise your name, for you will bring this time and you will bring it soon. For your kingdom must come, your will must be done on earth as in heaven, and everything must go according to your plan. Amen.

30
November

Shout for joy to God, all the earth! Sing the glory of his name; make his praise glorious...Come and see what God has done, his awesome deeds for mankind!

PSALM 66:1–2, 5

Lord our God, let your miracles be done among us, and bless us through your deeds. Bless us in Jesus Christ, the Savior of so many people. May your kingdom come to us and at last bring the great miracles that carry out your will and that do what is pleasing to you. Lord God, Father in heaven, we praise you! In you we live, in you we believe, in you we hope, in you we want to live day by day and hour by hour. May your name be honored among us, for you are our God and the God of all the world. Let your light shine among all people so that many millions and whole nations may glorify your name, for in the last days the nations shall come and worship you. So protect and bless us today and in the coming time, and again and again let something happen to bring us new life and strength. Amen.

December

1

December

Say to Daughter Zion, "See, your king comes to you, gentle and riding on a donkey, and on a colt, the foal of a donkey"... The crowds that went ahead of him and those that followed shouted, "Hosanna to the Son of David! Blessed is he who comes in the name of the Lord! Hosanna in the highest heaven!" MATTHEW 21:5, 9

Lord our God, we thank you for letting hosannas rise from people's hearts and for letting us cry out to you all the more fervently in dark times. Help us, O Almighty God, and help your king, Jesus Christ, to his final victory. For he shall be victor, bringing grace, peace, life, and victory for all that is good, on earth as in heaven. He shall be victor at all times in our lives, enabling us to keep faith in trouble, fear, and need, yes, even in death. Hosanna to the victor, Jesus Christ, the victor you have chosen! O Almighty God, proclaim him on earth. Let all the people know he is on his way, to the glory of your name. Amen.

2

December

The Lord has done it this very day; let us rejoice today and be glad. Lord, save us! Lord, grant us success! Blessed is he who comes in the name of the Lord. From the house of the Lord we bless you. PSALM 118:24–26

Lord God, our hearts are full of praise and thanks for your promise. You comfort and help us with this promise every day, enabling us to hold true through all distress. Remember us in these times, and let the cry, "Hosanna," arise often in our hearts. Let a bright light shine out now as you once let it shine around the Lord Jesus, showing him as King and Savior. Protect us and bless us. Bless our land and all those appointed to govern. May your Spirit be with them so that they may carry out your will. For your will must be done and shall surely happen. In this we trust, and in this we hope. We praise you, O Lord our God. Hosanna! Hosanna in the highest! Amen.

3
December

And you, my child, will be called a prophet of the Most High; for you will go on before the Lord to prepare the way for him, to give his people the knowledge of salvation through the forgiveness of their sins, because of the tender mercy of our God, by which the rising sun will come to us from heaven to shine on those living in darkness and in the shadow of death, to guide our feet into the path of peace. LUKE 1:76–79

Lord our God, we thank you that you let light shine out every day and every year. Thank you that we may always look to you, whose right hand will bring order into everything and set all things right, even in difficult times. May our hearts receive strength to persevere and go on praising you, for you remain, no matter what happens on earth. You are our God, you have sent us the Savior, and we can draw close to you. You have made us the firm promise that your day is coming when truth and justice will arise on earth to the glory of your name. May the hearts of many people turn to you so that they worship you and call to you for help, to the glory of our Savior Jesus Christ. Amen.

4

December

Since you have kept my command to endure patiently, I will also keep you from the hour of trial that is going to come on the whole world to test the inhabitants of the earth. I am coming soon. Hold on to what you have, so that no one will take your crown. REVELATION 3:10–11

Lord our God, strengthen our hearts today through your Word. You are our Father and we are your children, and we want to trust you in every aspect of our lives. Protect us on all our ways, and grant that we may always watch and wait for the coming of your kingdom, for the future of our Lord Jesus Christ. Keep us from becoming confused by present-day events. Help us to remain free, that we may serve you and not be led astray, no matter what happens in the world. Grant us your Holy Spirit in everything, for without your Spirit we can do nothing. Help us, and accept our praise for the many ways you have given us help. Amen.

5
December

Then the sovereignty, power and greatness of all the kingdoms under heaven will be handed over to the holy people of the Most High. His kingdom will be an everlasting kingdom, and all rulers will worship and obey him. DANIEL 7:27

Lord our God, dear Father, you have made yourself known on earth so that we may love you and be loved by you. Give us your Spirit, we pray. Give us your Spirit to strengthen us in the life and work you offer us. Watch over us on all our ways. Wherever your children are sighing and calling for you, protect and guide them with your mighty hand. Let your kingdom spread over the whole world, over all people, over all races and nations, that we may become united as servants of Jesus Christ to your honor. Amen.

6

December

The Spirit and the bride say, "Come!" And let the one who hears say, "Come!" Let the one who is thirsty come; and let the one who wishes take the free gift of the water of life. REVELATION 22:17

Lord our God and Father in heaven, be with us and let your face shine upon us, for we are your children. In the midst of all human planning we are your children who seek you alone, who seek your will, your kingdom, and everything you have promised to humankind. Fill our thoughts and feelings with your power so that our lives on earth may belong to you, so that with our whole will we may put everything we have and are into your hands. For we want to be your children, to have one will with you, Almighty God. We want your kingdom. This is our will, O Lord our God, and it is your will too. Therefore it must come to pass, to the glory of your name. Amen.

7
December

In the last days the mountain of the Lord's temple will be established as the highest of the mountains; it will be exalted above the hills, and peoples will stream to it. Many nations will come and say, "Come, let us go up to the mountain of the Lord, to the temple of the God of Jacob. He will teach us his ways, so that we may walk in his paths." The law will go out from Zion, the word of the Lord from Jerusalem. MICAH 4:1–2

Lord our God, we gather in your presence, coming from this world so full of suffering, grief, and misfortune that we could well be afraid. But we do not have to rely on this world. We can come to you, the almighty God. You are our Father, and no matter what may come, we remain your children and receive your blessing. So protect us in this present time. Even if a flood of evil seems about to break over us and our hearts are heavy, you will uphold us. You will strengthen us so that we can bear this time patiently, hoping in you and in what you do for all people, who are your people just as we are. May the praise of your name be in our hearts for ever and ever. Amen.

8

December

And will not God bring about justice for his chosen ones, who cry out to him day and night? Will he keep putting them off? I tell you, he will see that they get justice, and quickly. However, when the Son of Man comes, will he find faith on the earth? LUKE 18:7–8

Father in heaven, we surrender ourselves to your love, the love in which Christ comes to us. Like children we say every day to the Lord Jesus himself, "Lord Jesus, come, come! Even if we cannot see you today because times have changed, come into the world, come more and more into world history. Send more and more of your nature, your goodness, into all hearts. Come at last, come quickly to bring an end to the adversary, an end to world power with its sinister, hostile character. May bright day, clear light from the Father in heaven, dawn through you, Lord Jesus. Yes, come, Lord Jesus!" Amen.

9
December

But if from there you seek the Lord your God, you will find him if you seek him with all your heart and with all your soul. DEUTERONOMY 4:29

Lord our God, we seek your face and long to find you. May we find you as your people found you in times past when you drew near with many signs and miracles. May our hearts come before you in awe and trust and draw their strength from you. May many in our time seek you and receive your comfort and help, for you provide strength and courage for the poor and destitute, for the suffering and the dying. Do not let our age pass by in vain, O great and almighty God. A new time must surely come, a new day must be born from this present age. This is your will, and in your will we trust. Amen.

10

December

But for you who revere my name, the sun of righteousness will rise with healing in its rays. And you will go out and frolic like well-fed calves. MALACHI 4:2

Lord our God, we think of all the people who have trusted in you. We remember all the signs and wonders you have shown to establish your name among us. We belong to those who hold to you today; may our hearts be kept faithful through your Spirit. Even if there are great hardships in our times and everything seems on the verge of collapse, even if the world perishes, you, O God, are our stronghold. This truth remains forever. In you we want to hold true until your great day comes, until the power of the Savior is revealed in many people so that in their misery they can believe and find help and comfort. Amen.

11
December

Keep me safe, my God, for in you I take refuge. I say to the Lord, "You are my Lord; apart from you I have no good thing." PSALM 16:1–2

Dear Father in heaven, look on us as your children, and grant that we may feel in you the highest good for time and eternity. Even if we have to deny ourselves and make great sacrifices, you remain our treasure, our riches, our love, and our joy. Give us strength as a gathered people ready to serve you. Grant us your Spirit whenever we do not understand what we should do. Shelter us always in your hands, and allow us to see your miracles in souls and in bodies. For you are our God, the Almighty, and you find the way to help in everything. Amen.

12

December

He came to that which was his own, but his own did not receive him. Yet to all who did receive him, to those who believed in his name, he gave the right to become children of God. JOHN 1:11–12

Lord our God, we thank you for allowing us to be called your children. We thank you for giving us the power to become more truly your children, so that there may be a witness to your name on earth, so that again and again in the name of Jesus Christ new power may come for body and soul, for the happy and unhappy, for all who are still following false paths, for all who suffer so much grief, fear, and need. We thank you and we praise your name. Help us on our way. Help us weak people who often grow anxious and afraid. Help us in everything. Help us especially in the concern we have deepest in our hearts, that your name may be honored, your kingdom come, and your will be done on earth as in heaven. Amen.

13

December

I will give you a new heart and put a new spirit in you; I will remove from you your heart of stone and give you a heart of flesh. And I will put my Spirit in you and move you to follow my decrees and be careful to keep my laws.

EZEKIEL 36:26–27

Lord our God, may our lives be awakened, for you send your Spirit to blow through heaven and earth and you stir everything to life. May we long for your Spirit's prompting. Grant that we not be overpowered by evil and sin. May we be born anew to be fighters for the highest good on earth, which leads into heaven. Hear the prayers of all people far and near who are sighing for the Savior. We pray for them all as we pray for ourselves, and you will hear our prayer. You will send power to lift up their hearts and souls so that there may be a great throng of your joyful people on earth. In spite of all the misfortune, adversity, and danger in the world, there will be a people exulting from one end of the earth to the other, a people trusting in you and sure of victory through the great grace you give in answer to our prayers. Amen.

14
December

Jesus Christ is the same yesterday and today and forever.

HEBREWS 13:8

Thank you, Father in heaven, for gathering us together and opening a door which can be entered by all who are like children. You open the door for all who have the childlike hope that you are carrying out your purpose, that in the midst of the ruin and sin of world history, life remains, the life of the Lord Jesus Christ, life for all the world. No one can destroy this life, which will soon gather power until all people see him, Jesus Christ, who for the salvation of humankind is the same yesterday, today, and in all eternity. Amen.

15
December

A voice of one calling: "In the wilderness prepare the way for the Lord; make straight in the desert a highway for our God. Every valley shall be raised up, every mountain and hill made low; the rough ground shall become level, the rugged places a plain." ISAIAH 40:3–4

Lord our God, open our ears and our hearts so that we hear you speaking and can follow the voice that cries out to us. May we be a people who prepare the way for you. Grant each of us strength to give up everything and to realize, "The way to my heart should be leveled too." The light is now shining for us in Jesus Christ, and through hearing his voice we will find strength and help. Help will be very near to us, and the mighty hand of the Lord Jesus will be over us in every need. For this he came. We can believe in his help, and we long for it. Hear the inmost longing of each of us, and make us part of your people so that we may keep hope in our hearts and serve you on earth. Praise to your name, O Father in heaven, that you have put us on earth and that we can draw strength from the One who fights and is victorious, Jesus Christ. Amen.

16

December

The Sovereign Lord has given me a well-instructed tongue, to know the word that sustains the weary. He wakens me morning by morning, wakens my ear to listen like one being instructed. ISAIAH 50:4

Lord our God, we thank you for giving us the task of serving you in the name of your servant, Jesus Christ, for letting each of us have a part in carrying out your will. Keep us true to this service. We want to be faithful, always listening to you, for you open our ears and help us know your will and respond to it. Be with us in these days. Strengthen your love and compassion in all hearts. May the life of Jesus Christ gain greater and greater power in all people on earth. Amen.

17

December

The life appeared; we have seen it and testify to it, and we proclaim to you the eternal life, which was with the Father and has appeared to us. I JOHN 1:2

Lord our God, we thank you that you have given us the light of life, that we can now learn how to live, and that through your great grace we may understand life in direct relationship with the Lord Jesus, who was crucified and who rose from the dead. Grant that the power of Christ may be made visible in us. Grant that his life may become our life, that we may leave behind all doubts and anxiety, even though we are often surrounded by darkness and night. Keep us in your Word. Let your will hold sway over all the world, for your will must be done in heaven, on earth, and down to the lowest depths. Let your will be done on earth as in all the heavens. Amen.

18

December

Praise awaits you, our God, in Zion; to you our vows will be fulfilled. You who answer prayer, to you all people will come. PSALM 65:1–2

Lord our God, our Father, out of reverent silence comes the praise that is due to you, O God in Zion. It is right for us to praise you and to keep our promises to you. People everywhere shall come to you, for you answer prayer. Protect us your children in the task you have given us. Watch over us so that we can serve you in the right way and receive from you the gifts we need in order to go toward your kingdom and witness to your name. Help us on every step of the way. May our lives be entrusted to your hands, and may we always find our strength in you, our God and Savior. Amen.

19

December

When the Lord restored the fortunes of Zion, we were like those who dreamed. Our mouths were filled with laughter, our tongues with songs of joy. Then it was said among the nations, "The Lord has done great things for them." The Lord has done great things for us, and we are filled with joy. PSALM 126:1–3

Dear Father in heaven, we hope in you and in your promise, which we hold in our hearts as our most precious possession. Protect us when times grow hard. May your Spirit come. May your Spirit constantly reveal your Word and give your promise to the hearts of many so that they may share in the hope, the faith, and the struggle for the great day. On that day we will be allowed to rejoice, exulting with all people because your salvation comes for the whole world. Amen.

20

December

This is the one about whom it is written: "I will send my messenger ahead of you, who will prepare your way before you." MATTHEW 11:10

Lord our God, thank you for bringing us into glorious day. Let the rays of your grace, the grace of Jesus Christ, shine into our hearts so that we are truly born of the Spirit and serve you as your children at all times, also when hard days come. Through your might and your revelation pry us loose from all earthly things. Pry us loose from worries and from pleasures. We are your children, O Lord God. We come before you, our Father in heaven, and you will accept us so that we may be a people who prepare the way for you. May all the words you speak be a blessing to us and make us joyful in expectation for the day of Jesus Christ, which has begun in power and glory and will bring power and glory when all is fulfilled according to your merciful and perfect decree. O God, your children entreat you, "Accept us. Hear us. Set the light aflame in our hearts for the coming of your great day!" Amen.

21
December

He received honor and glory from God the Father when the voice came to him from the Majestic Glory, saying, "This is my Son, whom I love; with him I am well pleased." We ourselves heard this voice that came from heaven when we were with him on the sacred mountain.

2 PETER 1:17–18

Lord Jesus Christ, to you we may lift our eyes, for you have broken free from our world of death and live in the glory of life, and you offer your life to us on earth. Let the power of your life be revealed today in us and in many others who want to celebrate Christmas. Send your Spirit to move our hearts so that we hear, see, experience, and understand what you and your gift of eternal life truly mean for us. So watch over us in these days and strengthen us in faith. Shed the light of your grace over us and within us. Protect us as your disciples. Lead us into communion with our Father in heaven and into community with you, O Jesus Christ, for all eternity. Amen.

22

December

Rejoice in the Lord always. I will say it again: Rejoice! Let your gentleness be evident to all. The Lord is near. Do not be anxious about anything, but in every situation, by prayer and petition, with thanksgiving, present your requests to God. And the peace of God, which transcends all understanding, will guard your hearts and your minds in Christ Jesus. PHILIPPIANS 4:4–7

Dear Father in heaven, let your joy be always in us, your children. Let your joy bring light and peace to our lives, no matter what happens around us. May we serve you in joy, aware of your peace at all times, so that something of this peace may go out from us to grieving hearts and to regions of the world that are in darkness. Father in heaven, how many unhappy people look up without knowing where to find help! But you will come to them. We beseech you, come to those who mourn, and let them find joy and trust for their redemption in Jesus Christ. Amen.

23
December

May our Lord Jesus Christ himself and God our Father, who loved us and by his grace gave us eternal encouragement and good hope, encourage your hearts and strengthen you in every good deed and word.

2 THESSALONIANS 2:16–17

Lord our God, our Father in heaven and our Father on earth, our Lord and our Ruler, we thank you that to this very day you have guarded and guided us and delivered us from great need. We praise you with hearts full of hope as we continue on our pilgrimage. For Christmas Day is coming with its message of hope that we may somehow bring honor to you in spite of all hindrances, mistakes, and sin, in spite of all death and the horror of dying. We know that you hold us in your hands. With your help we can look ahead, and again and again we may take a small step forward and live to the praise and honor of your name. So be with us now and bless us. Amen.

24

December

But the angel said to them, "Do not be afraid. I bring you good news that will cause great joy for all the people. Today in the town of David a Savior has been born to you; he is the Messiah, the Lord"...Suddenly a great company of the heavenly host appeared with the angel, praising God and saying, "Glory to God in the highest heaven, and on earth peace to those on whom his favor rests." LUKE 2:10–11, 13–14

Lord God, our Father in heaven, you have sent us the Savior, who was born to bring great joy to all people. Glorify your name, we pray. Give the world the peace you alone can give, the peace that wells up in our hearts. Let your favor rest on us so that we may hold out under our sufferings on earth. We need your loving help to remain inwardly steadfast until everyone can be reached by the message, "Be strong in the grace of Jesus Christ." Amen.

25
December

For to us a child is born, to us a son is given, and the government will be on his shoulders. And he will be called Wonderful Counselor, Mighty God, Everlasting Father, Prince of Peace. ISAIAH 9:6

Lord our God, you have sent light to shine on earth and have revealed your heavenly power in Jesus Christ, so that in spite of all darkness and evil we may rejoice because we have a Savior. Reveal your power in our day. Let something be done anew toward the building of your kingdom on earth. Draw all hearts to you and give them light, so that they may thank and praise you for all you have done and are doing to bring the whole world into your hands. O Lord God, let people be moved by the opening of the heavens. May their hearts awaken and their sadness give way to joy in Jesus Christ the Savior. We, your children, wait in expectation for you to set everything right. We know that even in our troubled times your hand is at work to reveal your will to all generations, as you promised through Abraham. May your name be honored, your kingdom come, and your will be done on earth as in heaven. Amen.

26
December

For God so loved the world that he gave his one and only Son, that whoever believes in him shall not perish but have eternal life. JOHN 3:16

Lord our God, our light and our life, in our longing to live by your Word we lift our eyes to you. Let your Word come into our hearts. Let your Word help us to understand our lives and our time, so that we can recognize your leading in everything and gather courage every day in spite of our weakness, sins, and faults. We can still find joy, for your kingdom is coming. We can feel that you are among us, however great the anguish of these times. Let the light of Jesus Christ shine out; let your Spirit of peace and grace come to all nations so that your will may be done. Free people from all their confusion. Release them from their bondage. Make them free for what is good, true, and eternal. May your name be praised among us today and forevermore. Amen.

27
December

Praise be to the Lord, the God of Israel, because he has come to his people and redeemed them. He has raised up a horn of salvation for us in the house of his servant David. LUKE 1:68–69

Lord our God, dear Father in heaven, we come into your presence and ask you to show yourself to us as the true, great, and almighty God, who can shed light into our misery and change it all, letting us find reconciliation and redemption in Jesus Christ. Protect and help us with your mighty hand. Let every country and nation see your grace and see the victory over all sin and injustice. Let your justice come on earth, and let peace fill every heart and show in every life. May all that happens to us serve the good. Help us always look to you, our Lord and God, for you have power to rule everything and to turn everything to its right purpose. Amen.

28

December

But when the set time had fully come, God sent his Son, born of a woman, born under the law, to redeem those under the law, that we might receive adoption to sonship.

GALATIANS 4:4–5

O Lord God, we thank you for everything you allow us to see and hear. May our hearts become awake and alive through all we receive so that we await your final revelation and recognize your ultimate will for all people, for all nations and races on earth. Hear us in these days, for we know your kingdom is coming. Your kingdom is before our eyes. Your Word, your help, is coming, and in Jesus Christ light will dawn for all the world. Praise and honor to you for all you do! May we see it all before our eyes so that our expectation of the last days is a living expectation, full of joy and blessing. We want to wait in joy, in love, and in longing for the day that is coming to your glory. Amen.

29

December

Praise the Lord. Give thanks to the Lord, for he is good; his love endures forever. PSALM 106:1

Dear Father in heaven, whose might is over all the earth, we thank you for all the love you show us. We also thank you for everything that seems hard, but which you change into help and strength. We want to thank you in life and in death, in joy and in sorrow, for you are the great and mighty God, who calls us to life again and again, who leads us to fuller life. You have given us great love in Jesus Christ, our Savior. He shall always be before our eyes and remain in our hearts. Through him we can cry out in joy, "Abba, dear Father!" Amen.

30

December

And Mary said: "My soul glorifies the Lord and my spirit rejoices in God my Savior, for he has been mindful of the humble state of his servant. From now on all generations will call me blessed, for the Mighty One has done great things for me – holy is his name." LUKE 1:46–49

O Lord God, in exultation our hearts go out to you and your revelation of heaven, your revelation of the Spirit, who can fill our hearts so that we remain steadfast throughout our earthly life. It is still dark on earth. Sin and death hold sway, but we stand unafraid and seek repentance. In spite of all our failures we look to you and know you are our Savior. You send us Jesus Christ in your own glory. The world will be filled with light. Everywhere on earth, even among those who do not know you, the sincere-hearted will come to acknowledge that you, the Father of Jesus Christ and our Father, are God over all the world. You will show your glory to all people so that they may come to you, worship you, and walk in the light, to the everlasting glory of your name. Amen.

31
December

In the beginning you laid the foundations of the earth, and the heavens are the work of your hands. They will perish, but you remain; they will all wear out like a garment. Like clothing you will change them and they will be discarded. But you remain the same, and your years will never end. PSALM 102:25–27

Lord our God, thank you for letting your light shine every day of every year. Thank you that we may always lift our eyes to you, whose right hand will bring true order to everything, even in difficult times. Give our hearts the strength to be faithful in this age, the strength to glorify you. For you remain, no matter what happens on earth. You are our God. You have sent us the Savior and we can draw close to you. Your promise to us stands firm, the promise that your day with its truth and justice shall come, to the honor of your name. May many people turn their hearts to you; may they worship you and call to you for help, to the glory of our Savior Jesus Christ. Amen.

Other titles in this series:

Watch for the Light

Readings for Advent and Christmas

Dietrich Bonhoeffer, Annie Dillard, Thomas Merton, Kathleen Norris, C. S. Lewis, Henri Nouwen, and others

These fifty devotions invite the reader to contemplate the great themes of Christmas and the significance that the coming of Jesus has for each of us – not only during Advent, but every day. Whether dipped into at leisure or used on a daily basis, *Watch for the Light* gives the phrase "holiday preparations" new depth and meaning.

Bread and Wine

Readings for Lent and Easter

Wendell Berry, G. K. Chesterton, Blaise Pascal, Dorothy Sayers, John Updike, Oscar Wilde, and others

A time for self-denial, soul-searching, and spiritual preparation, Lent is traditionally observed by daily reading and reflection. This collection will satisfy the growing hunger for meaningful and accessible devotions. Culled from the wealth of twenty centuries, the selections in *Bread and Wine* are ecumenical in scope, and represent the best classic and contemporary Christian writers.

Lightning Source UK Ltd.
Milton Keynes UK
UKHW02f0819240418
321518UK00003B/42/P

9 780874 860979